S0-BFB-549

SEATTLE'S
CELEBRITY
CHEFS

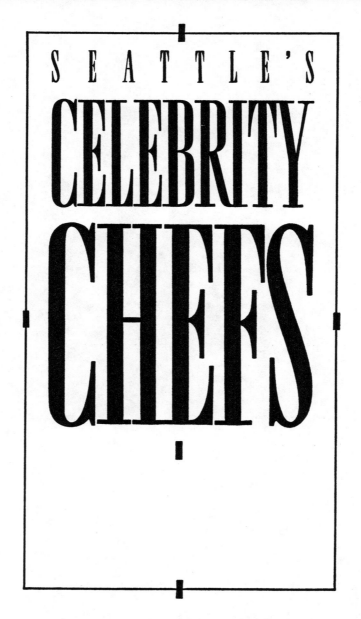

SEATTLE'S
CELEBRITY CHEFS

Sponsored by Henry's Off Broadway
Proceeds benefit Children's Orthopedic Hospital and Medical Center
by Mike McCormack and Bill Schwartz

Introduction by *Entertainment Tonight's*

Robb Weller

PEANUT BUTTER
PUBLISHING

PEANUT BUTTER PUBLISHING
SEATTLE, WASHINGTON

First Printing—April, 1986
Second Printing—July, 1986

Copyright © 1986 by Peanut Butter Publishing.
All rights reserved. No portion of this book may be
reproduced without written permission from the
publisher.

Peanut Butter Publishing
911 Western Avenue
Suite 401 Maritime Building
Seattle, WA 98104

ISBN 0-89716-149-1

ACKNOWLEDGEMENTS

Many thanks go to the people who worked so hard to make *Seattle's Celebrity Chefs* a reality.

Special thanks to all of the Celebrities who shared their favorite recipes with us.

Project managers Cindy Craig and Jane Stabelfeldt of The Butcher Restaurant Organization, who were responsible for editing and cookbook production.

Patty Oscar and the members of the Evelyn Wylde Guild of Children's Orthopedic Hospital and Medical Center who made many contacts to the Celebrities.

COHMC Board Members Kate Webster and Helen Stusser, and staff members Debra Holland and Lois Harris, who provided invaluable assistance and support.

And Tim Girvin of Tim Girvin Design for designing the cover of *Seattle's Celebrity Chefs*.

Color Litho'd by Trucolor.

CONTENTS

For more than 15 years The Butcher Restaurant Organization has been involved in various ways in the support of our community. Sponsoring *Seattle's Celebrity Chefs* to benefit Children's Orthopedic Hospital and Medical Center is a wonderful opportunity to show our appreciation for what Children's does for all of us in the Seattle area. We are proud to live in a city where our most precious resource, our children, can receive the special care and treatment they uniquely require.

We have been personally touched recently by Children's Orthopedic Hospital and the special consideration and care they give to their "little patients." All of us associated with Henry's Off Broadway have been grateful for the high level of professionalism and concern shown by the doctors and the staff at Children's toward the daughter of one of our own Executive Chefs during her treatment there.

The proceeds from the sales of *Seattle's Celebrity Chefs* will be contributed to Children's Orthopedic Hospital so that they can continue providing the finest care possible for sick and injured children.

I would also like to show my appreciation to my favorite Celebrity Chef, my mother, Claire Schwartz, by dedicating this book to her for all of the superb dishes she has so lovingly prepared and served over the years.

Bill Schwartz

Bill Schwartz
Honorary Chairman
Seattle's Celebrity Chefs

I left Seattle in the late 70's to pursue a career in broadcasting.
As a result, my work has taken me to Columbus, Ohio, Chicago,
New York and now Los Angeles. I love the hardiness of the Midwest,
the fast pace of the East and Hollywood's sense of the off-beat.
Nowhere have I found the spirit for helping others which exists
in the Puget Sound area.

Seattle's Celebrity Chefs cookbook typifies the help and love our
area so willingly puts forth. For this reason I am happy to be
a part of it. Children's Orthopedic Hospital and Medical Center
deserves all our efforts to further the reach of its caring arms.
If cooking up some delicious epicurian delight found in the
following pages helps to raise the much needed funds constantly
required, then we benefit in two ways. We can enjoy something
good for the soul and good for the palate.

My wholehearted thanks goes to you and the area known as God's
Country for responding to this Seattle's Celebrity Chefs cookbook.
However, since I have not sampled all the culinary attempts
contained herein, please don't blame me if you need to run for
the Bromo-Seltzer at 2 o'clock in the morning. After all, one
man's souffled chicken dumplings may be another's digestive Waterloo.

Cook in good faith, and always have faith in Children's. It is
a bright star of which we are all proud!

Robb Weller
CoHost
Entertainment Tonight

Children's Orthopedic Hospital and Medical Center is a private, non-profit facility which serves the special physical, emotional and social needs of sick or disabled children throughout the Pacific Northwest. It provides a full range of health care services for children from birth to 21 years of age and admits patients of all races and religions.

Last year, Children's provided over $11,000,000 in uncompensated care. Through various fund raising activities, over $2,000,000 was raised by 541 guilds composed of over 14,500 members. My wife, Ann, a member of the Paul Pigott Guild since 1983, has been involved in many fund raising projects. I am pleased, as Honorary Chairman, to add my support to yet another effort to continue fine quality care at Children's Orthopedic Hospital and Medical Center.

Mike McCormack

Mike McCormack
Honorary Chairman
Seattle's Celebrity Chefs

KIRO Newsradio 71

KIRO Television
KIRO Newsradio
KSEA Stereo

Broadcast House
Third Avenue & Broad Street
Seattle, Washington 98121
(206) 624-7077

Joseph K. Abel
Vice President/General Manager

Coquilles St. Jacques with Champagne Sauce

Serves 4
$\frac{1}{4}$ cup plus 2 tablespoons butter
1 shallot, chopped
1 cup brut champagne or white wine
salt & pepper (white)
$1\frac{1}{2}$ pounds scallops
$2\frac{1}{2}$-3 cups cream

Saute the two tablespoons butter and the shallot till soft.

Add the champagne and simmer till reduced by half.

Season with salt and white pepper.

Add scallops and top with a piece of buttered waxed paper. Simmer gently 2-3 minutes. Remove scallops and keep warm.

Increase heat and reduce sauce to a glaze.

Blend in cream. Simmer 20 minutes or till thickened.

Whisk in butter, cut into bits.

Garnish with sliced kiwi fruit if desired.

The Bonneville Group

FM Radio: KSEA, Seattle · WRFM, New York · KBIG, Los Angeles · WCLR, Skokie/Chicago · KOIT, San Francisco · KMBR, Kansas City · KAFM, Dallas.
AM Radio: KIRO-AM, Seattle · KBRT, Los Angeles · KMBZ, Kansas City · KSL, Salt Lake City.
Television: KIRO-TV, Seattle · KSL-TV, Salt Lake City.

Morris J. Alhadeff
President

"CHICKEN ala MORRIE"

2 medium fryers (cut up)	juice of 1 lemon
4 tbs. butter	1/2 lb. fresh mushrooms
1/3 cup olive oil	2 to 3 tbs. chopped parsley
1 cup white dry vermouth	salt and pepper to taste

Cut all chicken pieces in half again with cleaver, trim fat. Melt
butter and olive oil together in black iron skillet, or electric
skillet, until it froths. Reduce heat and saute' chicken pieces until
brown. When chicken pieces are nearly done add dry vermouth and lemon
juice. Continue cooking 10 minutes.

Meanwhile, place sliced mushrooms, chopped parsley and small amount of
butter or oil in iron pot which has been pre-heated in oven. Pour
chicken mixture over this, cover and return to oven 1/2 hour at 300 degrees.

Washington Jockey Club, Operators of **Longacres Race Track** P.O. Box 60, Renton, Washington 98057 (206) 226-31:

 PORT OF SEATTLE

Henry M. Aronson
Commissioner

I am very hard pressed to say what my singular <u>most</u> favorite recipe is, but one of my very favorites is the following very quick and simple one for clam soup:

    1 quart whole milk (can be varied or combined with skim or 2%
    milk or cream depending on ones affinity for richness and diet
    of the moment).
    2 cans minced clams
    "Thanksgiving spices" – thyme, sage, related available herbs
    butter
    onions
    green pepper
    salt, pepper and paprika
    sherry (optional)

    Combine milk (or milk and cream, etc.) with minced clams and
    spices in a soup pan and bring just short of boil – stir as
    needed to avoid sticking to bottom of pan.
    Simultaneously, melt butter in sauce pan and saute diced
    onions (until golden) and diced green peppers until warmed
    through but still crunchy.
    Add mixture of sauteed onions, peppers and residue of butter
    to milk and clams and stir.
    Season to taste with salt and freshly ground pepper.
    Serve in warmed cups or bowls, floating pad of butter and
    sprinkling paprika on top. Lace with a touch of sherry if to
    your taste.
    Serves four. Can be prepared from scratch in 10 minutes.

Enjoy!   All Best,

635 ELLIOTT AVENUE WEST • SEATTLE, WA • (206) 284-7220
MAILING ADDRESS: BOX C 19099, SEATTLE, WA 98109-1099
CABLE ADDRESS "DARIGOLD" SEATTLE TELEX 32-0015

Louis Arrigoni, President

COTTAGE CHEESE CHEESECAKE

1 cup graham cracker crumbs
2 Tblsp. DARIGOLD butter, melted
2½ lbs. (5 cups) DARIGOLD Large
    Curd Cottage Cheese
1 cup sugar
2 Tblsp. flour

6 DARIGOLD eggs
1 tsp. grated lemon rind
1 tsp. vanilla
1 pt. DARIGOLD Sour Cream
2 Tblsp. sugar

Allow all ingredients to come to room temperature. Line sides of 9-inch cheesecake pan with foil. Butter foil and bottom of pan. Mix crumbs and melted DARIGOLD Butter. Press evenly in bottom and around sides of pan. Chill. Sieve or put DARIGOLD Cottage Cheese in blender, about a cup at a time. Blend until smooth. Spoon into mixing bowl and combine with sugar and flour. Add DARIGOLD eggs, one at a time. Blend in rind and vanilla. Pour into prepared pan. Bake in 275 degree oven over 1½ hours or until filling is "set" on top. Center of filling will be soft. Combine DARIGOLD Sour Cream and sugar. Carefully spoon on top of cheesecake, spreading evenly. Bake 10 minutes longer. Cool. Refrigerate at least 5 hours. Before serving, carefully remove foil from sides of cake. Serves 10 to 12. Crushed sweetened fruit or berries may be served over slices.

Fresh Milk and Cream • Ice Cream • Butter • Cheese • Milk Powder • Evaporated Milk

The NBBJ Group

111 South Jackson Street
Seattle, Washington 98104
(206) 223-5555
Telex 329473 Burgess-Sea

Architecture
Interior Design
Planning
Economics
Cost Management
Graphic Design
Landscape Architecture

CAESAR SALAD   Six to eight servings

4	anchovies chopped, or equivalent in anchovy paste	2 or 3	bunches romaine, 3-8" long
1	egg	3 or 4	stalks of celery
1	teaspoon Worcestershire Sauce	½	teaspoon salt
½	teaspoon dry mustard	1	clove garlic, peeled
3	tablespoons red wine vinegar	3	tablespoons virgin olive oil
		1	lemon
		1½	cups croutons
		½	teaspoon freshly ground peppercorns
		1/3	cup freshly grated parmesan

Trim and wash the best inside leaves of romaine. Slice, don't tear, into large, bite size pieces. Spin dry. Wrap romaine and medium size pieces of celery in dish towel and chill in refrigerator along with plates, forks and wooden serving bowl. Mix 3/4 inch cubed pieces of French bread with fines herbs and melted butter or olive oil steeped in crushed garlic for several hours, then toast in oven. Whisk egg in small bowl, then add other ingredients in left hand column above.

Sprinkle bottom of chilled serving bowl with salt and rub with garlic clove. Press remaining garlic into dressing. Place romaine and celery in bowl, add olive oil and toss only enough to coat all leaves. Add dressing and toss again. Add croutons, squeeze lemon juice through cheese cloth, top with ground peppercorns and grated parmesan and give final toss.
Note: this is excellent with low fat cottage cheese on the side.

This recipe is part of a tradition that began at Cornell where one of my favorite professors held an open dinner discussion each Sunday night. Since he was unable to buy food for all of us, we brought our own ingredients and used his pots and pans. Many of us, certainly I with my Scottish background, brought a variety of hot cereals.

Later, back in Seattle and trying to find something healthy to feed four hungry boys, it seemed that hot cereal served with a really good Caesar salad would be the best way to fill them up. This slowly evolved into a strong tradition and is now what we almost always have on Sunday nights. The cereal is any one of a number of basic hot cereals including John McCann's Irish Oatmeal, Stone-buhr Hot Apple Granola, Red River Cereal from Manitoba and Snoqualmie Falls Lodge Oatmeal. The recipe on the box is supplemented with lots of dried fruit such as raisins, apples and apricots. Toppings are: bananas, strawberries, brown sugar, yogurt. For some reason, very few people accept our Sunday dinner invitations, but we still enjoy the tradition, especially when the making of the salad is started with a red wine toast to Caesar Cardini.

William Bain, Jr., FAIA
Partner

SEATTLE, WASHINGTON 98107   (206) 783-4851
CABLE ADDRESS: BARDAHL SEATTLE, TWX-910-44

O. BARDAHL
President

RUN WITH US

I emigrated from my native Norway to the Pacific Northwest in 1922. The next year I was able to send for my fiancee, Inga; we were married in 1924 and for over 60 years she has cooked wonderful meals for me and our family.

Because my business often takes me abroad, I have eaten in some of the world's finest restaurants but to me, Inga is still the best cook of all! When she makes her pancakes, friends and family eagerly stand in line for more. Here is my dear wife's own recipe for one of my favorites, Norwegian Pancakes.

NORWEGIAN PANCAKES
(serves 4)

In a mixing bowl, add all together and blend well the following ingredients:

        4 eggs
        2 c. milk
        1 tsp. salt
        2 Tbs. melted butter
        1 Tbs. sugar
        Just enough flour to make a <u>thin</u> batter.

For each pancake, grease a frying pan or skillet lightly, preferably with fresh bacon fat. Pour a small amount of batter into your pan, then tilt it so the batter covers the bottom of the pan. Fry until bubbles form all over the top of the pancake, then carefully turn and fry other side to a golden brown. You should now have a tender, almost paper thin pancake. Remove it to a clean surface, butter lightly, sprinkle with either regular or powdered sugar and roll up. Serve with bacon, ham or sausage and don't be surprised if each guest eats at least six of them!

Ole Bardahl

WORLD FAMOUS ADDITIVES AND LUBRICANTS

FAIRVIEW AVENUE NORTH AND JOHN STREET
POST OFFICE BOX 70
SEATTLE, WASHINGTON 98111

SEAFOOD DIJON
Serves 8

24 large shrimp, cleaned and peeled
1/2 lb. fresh local scallops
1/2 lb. fresh local mussels (lightly steamed & removed from
    shell; the 1/2 lb. figure is the meat alone)
2 Tbs. oil
1/2 onion, minced
1/2 c. dry white wine
1/2 c. heavy cream
2 sticks butter (1/2 lb.), cut in pieces
2 Tb. Dijon mustard

In a large skillet, saute the scallops and shrimp briefly until just undercooked. Remove them from the pan and set aside.

Saute the onion in the skillet until onion is translucent. Add wine and cream, stirring well; cook about 5 minutes over medium heat until mixture thickens enough to coat the back of a spoon.

Reduce heat to low and whisk in butter, then mustard. Add salt and pepper to taste Add the mussels and heat gently until they are warmed; then pour contents of the skillet over the shrimp and scallops in a serving dish (heated).

Serve at once. Excellent over rice or pasta; also good on its own.

-- Melinda Bargreen

U.S. ENVIRONMENTAL PROTECTION AGENCY
REGION 10
1200 SIXTH AVENUE
SEATTLE, WASHINGTON 98101

REPLY TO
ATTN OF: Ernesta Barnes

BRAISED FENNEL*

Fennel is somewhat like celery, but with a mild licorice flavor. The bulbs are available in local produce markets, from local growers in the summer and from California in the fall and winter. The stalks are available year round. One pound of fennel bulb serves three people.

Peel and quarter the bulb (cut in half if small). Melt enough butter in heavy saucepan to saute all pieces. Saute, turning each piece to brown lightly each side. Pour beef bouillon into the pan to 1/2 inch depth. Cover and simmer until tender (25-30 minutes).

Especially good served with creamed chip beef and baked potatoes.

*Good cooking does not have to be complicated. My menus include dishes I can prepare easily in the time available to a working mother with teenaged children.

BECKY BENAROYA

CHEESE PINWHEELS

1 cup oil
3/4 cup water
3 tsp. salt
1 1/2 cups grated kasseri cheese

Put all ingredients into large bowl. Stir and add enough flour
(approximately 3 cups) to make a soft dough. Do not knead, just
blend. Divide dough into 3 balls. Roll out dough one ball at
a time and sprinkle a little more cheese all over evenly and roll
into a log about 1 1/2 inches around.

Slice about 1/4 inch slices, lay flat on cookie sheet and sprinkle
grated Parmesan cheese.

Bake at 400 degrees for about 20 minutes or until golden brown.
Makes several dozen.

SEATTLE
SUPERSONICS

C Box 14102 — Seattle. WA 98114

STUFFED CHAYOTE SQUASH

3 medium chayote squash
½ cup celery, finely chopped
½ cup onion, finely chopped
½ cup bell pepper, finely chopped (red/green for color)
¼ cup parsley, chopped
1½ cup baby shrimp
2 cups bread crumbs
1 egg
salt
pepper
garlic powder
cayenne
parmesan

Steam squash until tender. Cut in half; remove the seed; scoop out the squash pulp (leave about ¼ inch inside the shell) set aside pulp and shell.

Saute in 4 T. butter: celery, onion and bell pepper and ¼ cup parsley.

When tender continue to add: baby shrimp, chayote pulp, 2 cups bread crumbs, 1 egg (slightly beaten). Season to taste with garlic powder, salt, pepper, and a dash of cayenne.

Fill the chayote shells with this mixture, sprinkle with parmesan cheese and bake at 350 for 25 minutes. Serves six.

"This is a wonderful old southern recipe I adopted from my mother-in-law. It is excellent for lunch accompanied by a green salad or it makes a great side dish for either beef or poultry."

                                    Bernie and Eugenia Bickerstaff

KIRO Newsradio 71

KIRO Television
KIRO Newsradio
KSEA Stereo

Broadcast House
Third Avenue & Broad Street
Seattle, Washington 98121
(206) 624-7077

SWEET AND SOUR FISH

1½-2 lbs white fish (Bass, Snapper, Sole, or Halibut) cut into serving
    pieces
1 teaspoon salt
1 piece ginger, pounded or may use ground ginger - smaller amount
4-6 Tablespoons flour
Saffola Oil to cover bottom of fry pan or wok

1. Rub fish with salt and ginger.
2. Sprinkle flour over fish.
3. Stir fry and drain fish.

Top with sauce: 1 cup water
    ¼ cup red wine vinegar
    ¼ cup sugar
    1 Tablespoon dark soy sauce
    4 Tablespoons shredded ginger, may use ground - smaller
      amount
    2 Tablespoons cornstarch dissolved in 2 Tablespoons cold
      water
    2 scallions, shredded
    ½ each red and green pepper, shredded

Put first 4 ingredients in pot. Bring to boil, add ginger. Simmer
over low heat 2 minutes. Thicken with cornstarch. Add scallions and
peppers. Bring to boil once more. Pour over fish immediately.

               Bob Blackburn

The Bonneville Group

FM Radio: KSEA, Seattle · WRFM, New York · KBIG, Los Angeles · WCLR, Skokie/Chicago · KOIT, San Francisco · KMBR, Kansas City · KAFM, Dallas.
AM Radio: KIRO-AM, Seattle · KBRT, Los Angeles · KMBZ, Kansas City · KSL, Salt Lake City.
Television: KIRO-TV, Seattle · KSL-TV, Salt Lake City.

The Seattle Times

F. A. BLETHEN
PUBLISHER AND CHIEF EXECUTIVE OFFICER

NEW YEAR'S DAY HOT CHILI

Enjoy this during the Rose Bowl halftime. A different and very tasty chili. I always make enough for everyone to have seconds. The sausage is a great addition and I always add extra! Beans are optional.

5 slices bacon
8 oz. link sausage, sliced
1½ lbs. beef chuck, diced
2 med. onions, chopped
1 green pepper, chopped
1 clove garlic, crushed
2 diced red chili peppers, seeded and crumbled
2 jalapeno peppers, seeded and chopped
1-1½ T. chili powder
½ t. salt
¼ t. dried oregano
2½ c. water
12 oz. tomato paste
16 oz. pinto beans

In a dutch oven cook bacon until crisp. Drain and crumble. Set aside. Brown sausage in pan. Drain sausage reserving 2 T. drippings. Set sausage aside. In reserved drippings brown diced beef, onion, green pepper and garlic. Add bacon and sausage, chili peppers, jalapeno peppers, chili powder, salt and oregano. Stir in water and tomato paste. Bring to boil. Simmer covered 1½ hours. Stir occasionally. Stir in beans. Simmer covered 30 minutes more. Serves 6-8 people.

Pass condiment dishes of shredded cheese, chopped onion, jalapeno peppers.

Joan Ross Bloedel

NEVER - FAIL FRUIT CAKE

This is my mother's and grandmother's recipe
for a delectable fruitcake. Raisins are the fruit
and oranges and spices are the flavors. Serve it
with hard sauce, whipped cream, ice cream, or plain.

2 cups boiling water
2 cups sugar
dash salt
1 teaspoon ground cloves
1 teaspoon cinnamon
1 box raisins
2 tablespoons butter
1 sliced orange

Boil above ingredients for 5 minutes. Remove orange
slices and squeeze out the juice.

Sift 3 cups of flour and 1½ teaspoons of baking soda
3 times; the third time sift over 3/4 cup of chopped
walnuts. Gently mix the flour and the nuts with two
forks.

Add ½ teaspoon lemon extract and ½ teaspoon orange extract
(or 1 teaspoon lemon) and pour into a greased and floured
tube pan.

Bake at 325 degrees for 45 minutes to 1 hour. Check with
a cake tester for slightly moist doneness.

Joan Ross Bloedel

Joan Ross Bloedel's sense of form, intertwined with her vivacious luminous
palette has become her trademark. Her monoprints, collages, and paintings
on paper reveal a poetic sensibility competently achieved through her
experimentation with materials and mastery of the media.

2207 East Republican Street
Seattle, Washington 98112
(206) 322-3034

BUTCH BLUM LASAGNE

1/2 lb spicy Italian sausage
1/2 lb mild Italian sausage
1 lb lean ground beef
1-2 tbsp basil
1-2 tsp salt
pepper to taste
2 cups diced tomatoes
2 6 oz cans tomato paste
1 8 oz can tomato sauce
3 cloves garlic, minced

Brown meat with garlic, drain fat. In a blender, combine tomatoes,

paste, sauce, and blend well. Add to meat mixture. Add basil, salt,

pepper. Simmer for 1 to 2 hours.

2 sheets lasagne verde (spinach pasta)
1/2 container of Ricotta cheese
1/2 cup grated Italian parmesan cheese
1 lb grated Italian Mozzarella cheese

In the bottom of a 9 x 12 lasagne dish, put 1/2 cup of sauce. Layer with

one lasagne sheet. Spread 1/2 of the Ricotta on the sheet. Then layer

1/2 of the mozzarella and meat sauce. Add second sheet, and then layer

ricotta, mozzarella and meat sauce again. Sprinkle Parmesan on top.

Bake at 375° about 35 minutes. Let stand for 10 minutes before serving.

Serves 8 portions.

BUTCH BLUM
1408 FIFTH AVENUE
SEATTLE, WASHINGTON 98101
TELEPHONE: (206) 622-5760

STUFFED ROAST HOFFMANN

This personal favorite my wife, Marlene, often serves our dinner guests, was an original specialty at the home of Karl Hoffmann, who was executive chef presiding over a menu of 37 entrees at Norm Bobrow's Colony during the launching of Pat Suzuki's singing career in the mid-50s.

---

3 lb rump roast
2 small carrots (diced)
½ tsp ground cumin
½ box frozen peas
1 clove minced garlic
1 tsp paprika
salt & pepper
flour
oil to fry
3 cups water

Choose a nice, rather rectangular piece of meat, and insert large holes, lengthwise, with a sharp knife. Separately, mix carrots, peas, cumin, garlic and salt to taste. Fill holes with this mixture and add more salt and pepper to the meat -- then roll meat into the flour and fry until brown. Add enough water to cover 3/4 of the roast, and cook in a heavy skillet on top of the stove at low temperature for 1½ hours. Take the roast from the skillet and slice crosswise in a way that the vegetables show through the holes. Meanwhile, make a light gravy with the meat's juice and put back the slices of roast. Simmer for 15 minutes and serve.

This is one of Phil's favorite recipes:

<u>Stuffed Pork chops and Glazed Apples</u>

Preheat oven to 350 degrees.

½ cup onion, finely chopped
¼ cup celery, chopped
1 medium apple, cored and coarsely chopped
¼ cup butter
3-4 slices of bread cut into ¼ inch cubes
¼ cup chopped parsley
1 3/4 teaspoons salt
1 egg
3 Tablespoons apple juice
6 thick pork chops
¼ teaspoon pepper
1 Tablespoon vegetable oil
1 to 1¼ cup chicken broth
1 Tablespoon cornstarch

<u>Glazed Apples</u>

2 Tablespoons butter
1 Tablespoon lemon juice
3 apples, thinly sliced
2 Tablespoons sugar

Saute onion, celery and apple in butter until tender. Remove from heat. Add bread cubes, parsley, 3/4 teaspoon salt and toss lightly. Combine egg and apple juice and add to bread mixture. Mix well until moistened.

Cut deep pockets in pork chops and rub pocket with remaining salt and pepper. Pack stuffing into pockets, fasten closed with toothpicks.

Brown chops in oil. Place chops, stuffing side up, in a cake pan. Cover with foil.

Bake in a preheated oven at 350 degrees for 30 minutes; remove foil. Add 3/4 cup of chicken broth. Bake uncovered for 30 minutes more.

Prepare Glazed Apples: Melt 2 Tablespoons butter. Add apples, 2 Tablespoons sugar and 1 Tablespoon lemon juice. Saute till tender and keep warm.

Make gravy with drippings and cornstarch dissolved in remaining chicken broth.

Arrange chops on platter with apples around the edges. Serve gravy on the side.

Phil and Ramona Bradley

Bernie's Famous Clam Linguine

1 large head garlic, peeled and thinly sliced
1 cup olive or vegetable oil or mix to taste
1 Tbsp. crushed, dried, hot pepper
ground white pepper, to taste
1 51 oz. can chopped clams
1 16 oz. jar clam juice
2 #'s linguine, preferably not fresh
chopped, fresh parsley
fresh, grated parmesan cheese

Fry sliced garlic in hot oil. When garlic browns, remove with pierced spoon. Be careful not to burn garlic. Keep fried garlic aside. Cool oil slightly. Add clams, dried red pepper and white pepper.

Crush crisp fried garlic into tiny pieces. Add to clam mixture.

Add clam juice as desired for looser sauce.

Cook atop stove at medium heat approximately 5 minutes. SAUCE is now made. Can be served immediately or refrigerate overnight.

Cook linguine al dente not more than 1 hour before serving. 1/2 hour before serving, heat sauce. Pour over linguine and heat in 350 degree oven 10 minutes or until very hot.

Put in server and sprinkle with fresh, chopped parsley.

Pass freshly grated parmesan cheese at table.

Serves 16 or more.

BERNIE'S (206) 722-8800

9800 40th AVENUE SOUTH, SEATTLE WASHINGTON 98118

Costco WHOLESALE ®
4401 4TH AVENUE SOUTH
SEATTLE, WA 98134-2311
TELEPHONE (206) 682-8909

CREME BRULEE

1 Quart Cream

1 Vanilla Bean

7 Ozs. Granulated Sugar

8 Egg Yolks

4 Ozs. Brown Sugar

Pinch Salt

Warm cream with vanilla bean and pinch of salt. Mix
sugar and egg yolks. Pour in cream and mix well.
Strain into a mold. Cook in another pan with a half-
inch of water for 30 minutes at 300°. Let cool for
30 minutes and spread brown sugar over Creme Brulee.
Glaze under broiler for 12 seconds.

Serves 6.

When my wife (Susan) thinks she has a
reason to be in trouble and needs to
soften me up this is what arrives at our Table
This dish will make Ivan The Terrible smile!

Jeff Brotman

BROUILLET'S CAPPUCCINO PARFAIT

Butterscotch Sauce

   1/2 cup butter
   1½ cups brown sugar
   1/8 t. salt
   2 T. white Karo syrup
   1/2 cup whipping cream
   1½ cups pecans
   1/2 t. cinnamon
   1 t. grated orange rind

Melt butter in saucepan; add brown sugar, salt and syrup.
Bring to boil and cook until sugar is dissolved. Gradually
add whipping cream, stirring constantly. Bring to boiling
point again. Cool. Add chopped pecans. Stir cinnamon and
grated orange rind into sauce. (Makes 1½ cups sauce.)

1/2 gallon coffee ice cream
Cool Whip

Alternate coffee ice cream, butterscotch sauce and cool whip
in 10 to 12 parfait glasses. Freeze until serving time. To
serve, top with cool whip and grated orange rind.

Old Capitol Building. FG-11. Olympia. Washington 98504

3

19

LAW OFFICES OF

BROWNE, RESSLER AND FOSTER

A PROFESSIONAL ASSOCIATION

650 COLMAN BUILDING

811 FIRST AVENUE

SEATTLE. WA 98104

(206) 624-7364

JOHN HENRY BROWNE. P.S.C.
ALLEN M. RESSLER. P.S.C.
JOANNE FOSTER. P.S.C.
DINA LAFAVE

SOLE PICCATA

Dip four fillets of very fresh sole lightly into a mixture of flour, salt and pepper. Shake off excess flour. Heat three-four tablespoons butter plus one tablespoon olive oil in a large skillet until bubbly but not brown. Saute fish lightly for two-three minutes on each side. Remove, drain all but two-three tablespoons of the butter/oil combination. Add two tablespoons vermouth and deglaze pan (keep this liquid in pan). Add three tablespoons capers, fresh, chopped parsley and swirl in two tablespoons whole butter. Return sole to pan and heat gently with sauce. Serve with fresh pasta with pesto.

PESTO

In a blender puree two cups fresh basil leaves, ½ cup pine nuts toasted, two gloves garlic (peeled and crushed), ½ teaspoon salt and ½ cup freshly grated Parmesan or Romano cheese. When thoroughly blended, remove from blender and beat in three tablespoons softened butter.

Freezes well.

THE CANLIS SALAD

This signature salad has found its way onto dozens of menus around America. It has been the hands down favorite of our guests for many years. We toss it tableside with a dressing of imported olive oil, lemon juice, coddled eggs and ground pepper.

RECIPE

Salad
1 large head Romaine
1-2 peeled tomatoes

Condiments
1/4 cup chopped green onion
1 cup freshly grated Romano cheese
1 cup rendered finely chopped bacon
2 Tbs. chopped fresh mint
1/4 tsp. oregano

Dressing
1/2 cup olive oil
the juice of 1 lemon
1/2 tsp. fresh ground pepper
1 coddled egg
1/3 cup croutons

Into a large bowl place the tomatoes, cut in eighths. Add the Romaine, sliced in 1-inch squares. Then add green onions, cheese, bacon, oregano and mint. To make the dressing, put the pepper, lemon juice and coddled egg in a bowl and whip vigorously. Then slowly add olive oil, whipping constantly and tasting as you do. Pour over salad and toss thoroughly. Add croutons and a sprinkle of Romano cheese last. Serves four to six.

Sincerely,

Chris B. Canlis
President

Wok Ginger Beef

1 lb. sirloin tip or flank meat
1/2 C. ginger root
3/4 C. scallions
3 T. corn oil

Marinade:

1 1/2 T. soy sauce
2 T. dry sherry
4-6 drops ginger extract
1 t. sugar
2 T. sesame oil
2 T. corn starch

Trim any fat from the beef and cut it across the grain, into slices 1/8" thick x 3/4" x 2"; marinate for 15-20 minutes; while the beef is marinating, peel the ginger root and slice it thinly; cut the scallions into 1" lengths.

Heat 2T. of the oil in the wok and, when hot, add the marinated beef (without draining) and stir briskly until the meat has evenly changed color-approximately 1-2 minutes; remove the beef to a warm platter and wash the wok with hot water (no soap); heat the remaining 1T. of the oil and add the ginger root and scallions; stir briskly for one minute; return the beef to the wok and stir for 1-2 minutes.

Remove to the heated platter and serve with rice and stir-fried vegetables of your choice. Serves four.

Gregory P. Canova
Gregory P. Canova

Thomas A. Catlin
Assistant Head Coach
Defensive Coordinator, Linebackers

HERBED CHICKEN CASSEROLE

(Betty & Tom Catlin)

3 cups cooked chicken breast cut into bite size pieces
1 medium onion chopped
4 stalks celery chopped
1 large can chow mein noodles
1 large can Pet milk
2 cans cream of chicken soup
2 cans cream of mushroom soup
2½ cups Pepperidge Farm herb stuffing
1 stick margarine
  salt & pepper to taste

Saute onion and celery in a little margarine. Mix with all the remaining ingredients except stuffing mix and margarine. Pour into 2 casseroles 9" x 13".

Melt margarine and toss with stuffing mix. Put on top of casseroles. Bake at 350° for 45 minutes.

Let stand a few minutes before cutting into squares for serving.

(serves 20)

Seattle Seahawks

5305 LAKE WASHINGTON BLVD • KIRKLAND, WA. 98033 • (206) 827-9777

ROD CHANDLER
8TH DISTRICT, WASHINGTON

COMMITTEES:
BANKING, FINANCE AND
URBAN AFFAIRS

EDUCATION AND LABOR

Congress of the United States
House of Representatives
Washington, DC 20515

216 CANNON BUILDING
WASHINGTON, DC 20515
(202) 225-7761

DISTRICT OFFICES:

3350 161ST AVENUE, SE
BELLEVUE, WA 98008
(206) 442-0116

1025 SOUTH 320TH
FEDERAL WAY, WA 98003
(206) 593-6371
(206) 941-2876

HEARTY BEEF SOUP

Legend has it that Senator Zachariah Chandler enjoyed a similar tasty dish in the 1860s in Michigan. Pioneers of the Chandler family carried it with them to the west where generations of the family have enjoyed it since.

1 pound chopped beef	2 teaspoons salt
1 cup chopped onion	1 tablespoon bottled brown
3 cups water	bouquet sauce (an ingredient
1 28 ounce can of tomatoes	added in the 20th century)
1 cup diced carrots	1/4 tablespoon black pepper
1 cup diced celery	1 bay leaf
1 cup cubed potatoes	1/8 teaspoon basil

In a large saucepan, cook and stir meat until brown. Drain off fat. Add onions, cook and stir. Stir in remaining ingredients, heat to boiling. Reduce heat, cover and simmer until vegetables are tender. Recipe makes six servings.

Sincerely,

Rod Chandler
Member of Congress

PISTACHIO SALAD

Mix together:

1 large package Pistachio Pudding Mix (dry)
1 large container Cool Whip
1 can (16 oz.) crushed pineapple (do not drain)
1½ cups miniature marshmallows
1 cup coconut

THE
CHILDREN'S
ORTHOPEDIC
HOSPITAL
AND MEDICAL CENTER

Shirley Cockrill

President, Board of Trustees

CHICKEN TARRAGON   (six servings)

1/2 to 1 Pound fresh mushrooms
1/4 - Cup butter
6   - Large chicken breasts
1   - Tablespoon Beau Monde seasoning
1   - Teaspoon dry tarragon
1   - Cup dry white wine
1   - Cup dairy sour cream
1/2 - Chopped green onions

Slice mushrooms and saute in 2 T butter until golden.
Remove mushrooms and reserve.
Add remaining butter to pan and brown chicken.
Sprinkle with Beau Monde during browning.
Add mushrooms, sprinkle with tarragon.
Pour wine over chicken.
Cover and simmer 45 minutes - until tender.
Remove chicken to platter and spoon sour cream into
   pan juices and heat, but do not boil.
Pour sour cream mixture over chicken and sprinkle
   with green onions.

Shirley Cockrill

P.O. BOX C5371 • 4800 SAND POINT WAY N.E. • SEATTLE, WASHINGTON 98105 • (206) 526-2000

KIRO Inc.

KIRO Television
KIRO Newsradio
KSEA Stereo

Broadcast House
Third Avenue & Broad Street
Seattle, Washington 98121
(206) 624-7077

WAYNE'S FAVORITE CHOCOLATE MOUSSE PIE

Crust: 3 cups chocolate wafer crumbs
         ½ cup unsalted butter, melted

Filling: 1 pound of semi-sweet chocolate
         2 eggs
         4 egg yolks
         2 cups of whipping cream
         6 T. powdered sugar
         4 egg whites (room temperature)

Topping: 2 cups whipping cream
         Sprinkle of sugar

Method

Crust: Combine crumbs and butter. Press on bottom and completely
         up sides of 10" spring form pan. Refrigerate 30 minutes or
         chill in freezer.

Filling: Soften chocolate in double boiler. Cool to 45 degrees (F)
                                             (lukewarm)
         Add whole eggs and mix well. Add yolks and mix until
         thoroughly blended. Whip cream with powdered sugar until
         soft peaks form. Beat egg whites until stiff but not dry.
         Stir a little of cream and whites into chocolate mixture
         to lighten. Fold in remaining cream and whites until com-
         pletely incorporated. Turn mixture into crust and chill
         at least six hours (preferably overnight). This can be
         frozen - thaw overnight in refrigerator if you freeze.

ıhe best pie you've ever tasted.

Wayne Cody

The Bonneville Group

FM Radio KSEA Seattle · WRFM New York · KBIG Los Angeles WCLR Skokie Chicago · KOIT San Francisco KMBR Kansas City KAFM Dallas
AM Radio KIRO-AM Seattle · KBRT Los Angeles · KMBZ Kansas City KSL Salt Lake City
Television KIRO-TV Seattle KSL-TV Salt Lake City

"ANTIC DIVERSIONS"

*Intimate, humorous,
instant theatre happenings*

Clayton Corzatte & Susan Ludlow

WHITE FISH
with lemon & parsley

Ingredients:

    2 lbs. 1/2 inch thick white fish fillets
       (halibut, cod, sole)
    4 large onions, chopped
    2-3 cloves garlic, minced
    1 LARGE fistful fresh chopped parsley
    2 peeled chopped tomatoes
    2 peeled sliced tomatoes
    1 blanched, thinly sliced lemon*
    1 scant cup white wine
    1/2 tsp. oregano

Directions:

    Sprinkle fish with salt, pepper & lemon juice.
    In olive oil, saute onions & garlic until soft.
    Add parsley & chopped tomatoes and simmer
     about 5 minutes.
    Sprinkle oregano over all.
    Put fish fillets in a single layer in an oven-to-
     table baking dish. Cover with vegetables.
    Pour in wine.
    Layer sliced tomatoes over top.
    Layer lemon slices over all.*

Bake:

    Covered at 325° for 30 minutes.

Serve:

    over rice. Serves 4.

*After blanching lemon, taste a piece of the rind.
If your lemon is bitter, squeeze the juice and use
it in place of the sliced lemon. The dish will still
be beautiful and delicious!

Quick and Easy Pork Chops and Rice Casserole

Add the following ingredients to a casserole
dish large enough to hold 4 pork chops:

  1 Can of Chicken Gumbo soup (10-3/4 oz.)

  1 Soup can of water

  1 Soup can of uncooked minute rice

Brown 4 pork chops, adding your favorite
seasoning. Place the pork chops on the top
of this mixture and bake uncovered in a
325° oven for 45 minutes.

This casserole along with a green salad and
applesauce makes an easy and tasty supper.

Donald J. Covey

School of Medicine
Office of the Dean

Growing up in Tennessee, I've always had a fondness for specialties from the South. Here's a favorite of mine.

Southern Pecan Tassies

Bake at 325 degrees for 25 minutes. Makes about 2 dozen tiny tarts. Quadruple recipe to serve 40 to 50.

Pastry: 1 - 3 ounce package cream cheese
         1/2 cup butter
         1 cup sifted all-purpose flour

Blend cream cheese and butter until smooth; add flour; blend well. Chill dough 2 hours or overnight.

Shape dough into 24 one-inch balls. Press into tiny (1 3/4 inch) ungreased muffin pans.

Filling: 1 egg
          3/4 cup packed brown sugar
          1 teaspoon vanilla
          1 tablespoon butter, melted
          2/3 cup chopped pecans

Blend egg, brown sugar, vanilla and butter. Stir in pecans. Pour into pastry shells. Bake at 325 degrees for 25 minutes. Cool before removing from pans.

I bet you will like them too!

Sincerely,

David C. Dale, M.D.
Dean

Fredric A. Danz

Submitted by: Mr. and Mrs. Fredric Danz

DILL-SQUASH CASSEROLE

2 lbs. small squash (yellow crookneck) sliced
½ large onion, sliced
2 tblsp butter
2 tblsp flour
1 cup sour cream
1 large Kosher dill pickle finely chopped

Cook squash in small amount of water until tender; drain well.
Saute onion in butter until tender. Add to squash. Add flour
and sour cream with 3/4 of the chopped dill pickle. Put in a
casserole dish and top with the remaining chopped dill pickle,
sprinkling generously with paprika. Heat thoroughly in the
oven at a low temperature (300°).

Regards,

Fred Danz
Fredric Danz

Mailing Address
600 106th N.E.·Bellevue, WA 98004   P.O. Box 91723·Bellevue, WA 98009
(206) 455-8120

FRED HUTCHINSON CANCER RESEARCH CENTER

Robert W. Day, M.D., Ph.D.
Director

SPINACH SALAD

Ingredients

1/2 tsp. dry mustard
fresh ground pepper to taste
3 T. vinegar
6 T. oil (safflower, or other low saturated fat)
2 artichoke bottoms, cooked and sliced
1 hard-boiled egg (white only)
1 tsp. chopped chives
1/4 c. plain, low fat yogurt
2 tsp. chopped parsley
1 bunch (approximately 4 cups loosely packed) and well-washed spinach

Mix mustard, pepper, vinegar, and oil, blending well. Add artichokes and
chives, toss lightly together and set aside to marinate for at least one hour
in the refrigerator. Blend the yogurt, chopped egg white, chives, and parsley
with the chilled marinade. Mix and toss with the spinach just before serving.
Alternatively, arrange the spinach leaves on a platter, spoon over the
contents of the marinade, reserving the artichokes (sliced) to a separate
condiment plate, and sprinkle the chopped parsley.

Serves 4-6.

Robert W. Day, M.D.
Director

DR. MARK DEDOMENICO   JOAN KING
SENIOR VICE PRESIDENT   HOME ECONOMIST

ROTINI CHICKEN SALAD

Perfect salad for potluck dinners. Serves a crowd.

Salad Dressing

1 cup mayonnaise
1/2 cup half and half
2 Tbsp. lemon juice
2 Tbsp. garlic flavored red wine vinegar
1 Tbsp. capers, drained
1/8 tsp. salt

Salad Ingredients

4 cups (approx. 2 lbs.) boned chicken breasts
1 tsp. pork and chicken seasoning
1/2 tsp. garlic powder
3 Tbsp. butter
1/4 cup dry white wine (Green Hungarian)
1 pkg. (12 oz.) MISSION Rotini
4 cups chopped fresh spinach
1 cup sliced green onions with tops
3/4 cup chopped parsley
1 cup slivered almonds, toasted
1 can (8 oz.) sliced water chestnuts, drained
2 tomatoes, cubed
Salt and pepper

Whisk salad dressing ingredients together and set aside. Sprinkle cubed chicken with pork and chicken seasoning and garlic powder. Saute chicken in butter for 5 minutes or until chicken is tender. Add 1/4 cup wine and simmer 3 minutes. Do not overcook. Cook Rotini according to package directions; drain and rinse in cold water. Combine Rotini with chicken and remaining ingredients except tomatoes. Gently toss with dressing; add tomatoes, salt and pepper to taste and toss again. Chill and serve. Makes 16 (1 cup) servings. If you wish to make a day ahead, save out spinach and add before serving.

MACARONI • SPAGHETTI • EGG NOODLES • SOUP • BEANS • RICE • GHIRARDELLI CHOCOLATE • COCOA & CANDY
Creators of Rice-a-Roni • Noodle-Roni • Stir'n Serv

33

Vitello Tonnato

I first had this dish on one of those perfect warm days on the Ligurian coast in Santa Margherita. We were in the third week of our trip and had finally dropped into the local pace. We were getting back to sensible eating and drinking habits, well almost. Since it was about 12:30 and we had had an espresso for breakfast, we stopped for lunch at our favorite restaurant. Had the great house white and an order of lasagne al pesto. Being still slightly hungry, I asked the waitress for a suggestion of something light and cool. Vitello Tonnato - veal with a tuna sauce. The best summer lunch around.

2 lbs top round of veal

1 can tuna in oil

3 eggs

lemons

anchovies

capers

olive oil

Trim all fat and skin off veal, tie and simmer for about 1 1/2 hr in water with onions carrots pepper and celery. Veal should be a little resistant to the fork - do not over cook as it's difficult to slice. Refrigerate. Make a heavy mayo with 3 yolks, juice of 1 lemon and slowly add 1 cup of olive oil - season with salt and cayenne. Set aside. In blender mix tuna, 5 anchovy fillets, 1/4 cup of capers and about 1/2 cup of oil to make the same consistency as the mayo that you are now going to blend together Thin slice veal and place on plate that has 1/4 of sauce spread on it, then cover veal with remaining sauce.

Peter

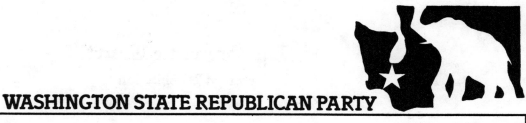
RASPBERRY BLUEBERRY SALAD
(Red, White, Blue Salad)

Layer I   -   Dissolve 1 small box of raspberry jello in a dish and let set.

Layer II   -   1 envelope plain gelatin in 1/2 cup of cold water.

Heat 1 cup of half & half milk, plus 1 cup of sugar - then mix in gelatin - add 1/2 tsp. vanilla & 8 oz. of Philadelphia Cream Cheese. Use mixer and beat well. While warm, add 1/2 cup of black walnuts. Pour this mixture over the first layer and let set.

Layer III -   1 small box of raspberry jello & 1 cup of hot water. Add 1 can of blueberry pie filling - cool and pour over second layer.

9 Lake Bellevue Drive
Bellevue, Washington 98005
(206) 451-1986

The Supreme Court
State of Washington

BARBARA DURHAM
JUSTICE
TEMPLE OF JUSTICE
OLYMPIA, WASHINGTON
98504-0511

(206) 753-5071

FRUIT PIZZA

CRUST

1	pkg	yellow cake mix
2/3	cup	graham cracker crumbs
1/2	cup	chopped nuts
1/2	cup	margarine or butter, softened
1	egg	

TOPPING

4 oz.	cream cheese	
1/2	cup	sugar
1 1/3	cup	whipping cream
	Assorted fresh fruit (sliced bananas, peaches, strawberries, blueberries)	
1/4	cup	apple jelly, melted

Heat oven to 350°F. In large bowl, combine cake mix, cracker crumbs, nuts and margarine at low speed until crumbly. Blend in egg. Press mixture in ungreased 12 or 14-inch pizza pan. Bake at 350°F for 15 minutes or until golden brown. Cool.

In small bowl, beat cream cheese until fluffy. Gradually add sugar; blend well. Beat in whipping cream until soft peaks form. Spread cream mixture on cooled crust. Arrange fruit as desired on top. Brush with melted jelly. Cut into wedges. Refrigerate leftovers.

12 or more servings.

Barbara Durham

Jean Enersen
333 Dexter Avenue North
PO Box 24525
Seattle, Washington 98124

STUFFED PUMPKIN

CLEAN OUT INSIDE OF 14" DIAMETER PUMPKIN (6-8LBS)
SPRINKLE INSIDE WITH WORCESTERSHIRE OR SOYA
SET PUMPKIN ASIDE TO MARINATE

STUFFING:
RICE (BROWN OR WILD)
MUSHROOMS (SAUTEED)
PUMPKIN SEEDS (ROASTED)
SUNFLOWER SEEDS (ROASTED)
ONION (SAUTEED)
APPLES & CARROTS
CHICKEN BROTH OR GARLIC
THYME, PEPPER, SAVORY

FILL WITH ANY OR ALL OF ABOVE INGREDIENTS
(ADD SAUSAGE, TURKEY OR CHICKEN IF YOU LIKE)
PUT LID BACK ON PUMPKIN
BAKE IN SHALLOW DISH
425 DEGREES FOR 1 HOUR

IT'S MARVELOUSLY FESTIVE LOOKING, FLEXIBLE ENOUGH
TO MEET MEATLESS OR SALTLESS DIET REQUIREMENTS
AND KIDS LOVE IT

United States Senate
WASHINGTON, D.C. 20510

CRAB LASAGNE

1/2 pound uncooked lasagne noodles
2 cans frozen shrimp soup, thawed
1 pound fresh Dungeness crabmeat
   (or 2 cans crabmeat)
2 cups small curd cottage cheese
6 ounces cream cheese

1 egg
2 teaspoons basil
1 medium onion, chopped
salt and pepper to taste
tomatoes, thinly sliced
cheddar cheese, shredded

Cook noodles 15 minutes. Combine soup with crabmeat and heat. Mix cottage cheese, cream cheese, egg, basil, onion, salt and pepper. In a baking dish, place a layer of noodles and cover with half of cheese mixture. Over this spread all of the mixed shrimp and crabmeat. Cover with remaining noodles and remaining cream cheese mixture. Top with tomato slices. Bake 15 minutes in a 350° oven. Sprinkle top with cheddar cheese and continue baking for 1/2 hour. Let set 10 to 15 minutes after it is baked to make serving easier. May be frozen. Makes 8 to 10 servings.

SENATOR DANIEL J. EVANS
United States Senator

KOLL

The Koll Company

2021 152nd Avenue, N.E.
Redmond
Washington 98052
(206) 643-1776

Rodger Fagerholm
Division President

PASTA WITH LOBSTER AND TARRAGON

A beautiful and sophisticated pasta dish, perfect as the first course of an important dinner. Begin with caviar or oysters, follow the pasta with Roast Veal or Filet of Beef, and fresh raspberries and cream.

        2 tablespoons best-quality olive oil
        1/2 cup finely chopped yellow onion
        1 can (2 pounds, 3 ounces) Italian plum tomatoes
        2 teaspoons dried tarragon
        salt and freshly ground black pepper, to taste
        1 cup heavy cream
        2 tablespoons salt
        1 pound spaghetti
        pinch of cayenne pepper
        1/2 pound lobster meat or more, about 1-1/2 cups,
            the equivalent of a 3 to 4 pound lobster
        parsley, fresh basil or fresh tarragon sprigs (garnish)

1. Heat the oil in a saucepan. Add the onion, reduce the heat and cook, covered, until tender, about 25 minutes.

2. Chop and drain the tomatoes and add them to the onions. Add the tarragon, season to taste with salt and pepper, and bring to a boil. Reduce heat, cover and simmer, stirring occasionally, for 30 minutes.

3. Remove the mixture from the heat and let it cool slightly. Puree it in the bowl of a food processor fitted with a steel blade, or use a food mill fitted with a medium disc.

4. Return puree to the saucepan, stir in heavy cream, and set over medium heat. Simmer the mixture, stirring often, for 15 minutes, or until slightly reduced. Taste the sauce, correct seasoning, and stir in cayenne and lobster meat. Simmer further, 3 - 5 minutes, or just until lobster is heated through.

5. Meanwhile, in a large pot, bring 4 quarts water to a boil. Add the salt, stir in the pasta, and cook until tender but still firm. Drain immediately and arrange on warmed serving plates. Spoon sauce evenly over pasta and garnish with a sprig of parsley, basil or tarragon. Serve immediately. 6 portions as a first course, or 4 as a main course.

    *Borrowed from The Silver Palate Cookbook. "Absolutely the finest PASTA sauce ever!"

Suite 800
1111 Third Avenue
Seattle, Washington 98101

AUSTRIAN GNOCCHI WITH CHICKEN
Pronounced "Knee-oh'-key"

This potato dumpling entree has been a favorite passed down from my mother's family. Her parents emigrated from Austria in the 1900's and settled in Tacoma. Frequently prepared by my Grandmother Kinkella and then my mother. The recipe was passed on to my wife, Barbara, who now prepares it for me and our children when we request it for special occasions such as birthday dinners. This recipe serves 5 or 6.

Part 1   Chicken & Sauce

    1 frying chicken cut into parts, or pieces of your choice to
        serve 6
    2 16 oz. cans tomato sauce
    1 6 oz. can tomato paste
    1 medium onion, diced
    1 tsp. salt
    2 tsp. Italian seasoning
    ½ tsp. pepper

Braise chicken pieces with diced onions. Add all other ingredients in a large kettle and simmer for 1½ to 2 hours. (The original recipe used stewing chicken. If you choose to use them, simmer 4-6 hours. It allows for a better chicken flavor in the sauce, but the meat is not as tender.)

Part 2

    5 medium white potatoes*
    About 4 or 5 cups flour
    1 egg
    Salt to taste

*(Short cut, use instant potatoes to serve 4, prepared according to package directions.)

Boil and mash potatoes, add salt and egg. Work in flour until dough is very stiff and not sticky, similar to bread dough consistency.

Separate into 2 or 3 sections. Roll each part on floured bread board into long strips about 1½ inches in diameter. Cut into 2 inch pieces and boil. They are done when they float on the surface.

Remove chicken pieces to serving platter and add Gnocchi to chicken sauce. Garnish with Parmesan cheese.
Serve with tossed salad

Word of caution: Gnocchi is not a "light meal". Be careful not to O.D.

Patrick M. Fahey
Patrick M. Fahey
President

EXECUTIVE OFFICE

CHARLES J. FERRARO
GENERAL MANAGER

Poached Quilcene Oysters with Red Bell Pepper Sauce:

6	large Quilcene oysters
¼ lb.	butter
1	red bell pepper
1 pint	whipping cream
1 cup	white wine
1 cup	fish stock
1	shallot
3 ozs.	butter
2 ozs.	mixed mushrooms
	spoonful of chives

Red Bell Pepper Sauce

Clean red bell pepper and cut into small squares. Chop shallot. Saute pepper and shallots in saucepan for approx. 3-4 mins. Add ½ cup white wine and reduce. Add 3/4 of the cream and cook for 15-20 mins. Blend entire mix in food blender to make the sauce. Season and keep warm.

Butter Sauce

Reduce one teaspoon of chopped shallot, add remaining cream and reduce. Over a very slow heat, add chives, seasoning and keep warm.

Cut mushrooms into uneven pieces. Saute with shallots and chives and keep warm.

Poach oysters in fish stock.

Composition of Plate

Pour red bell pepper sauce onto a dinner plate. Place drained poached Quilcene oysters in a circle and a tablespoon of cooked mushrooms in the center. With a teaspoon, coat each oyster individually with butter sauce.

Served with grilled garlic croutons.

FOUR SEASONS OLYMPIC HOTEL · SEATTLE

411 UNIVERSITY STREET, SEATTLE, WASHINGTON, 98101, USA. TELEPHONE (206) 621-1700, TELEX 00-152477

Four Seasons Hotels Montreal · Toronto · Ottawa · Calgary · Edmonton · Vancouver · New York (The Pierre) · Chicago (The Ritz-Carlton) · Dallas · Houston
Philadelphia · San Antonio · San Francisco (Clift) · Seattle (Olympic) · Washington, DC · Boston (1985) Inn on the Park Houston · London · Toronto

41

Good Company

A Production of KING Television   333 Dexter Avenue North   P.O. Box 24525   Seattle. Washington 98124   206/343-3781

GERMAN APPLE PANCAKE

This is my favorite brunch item for weekends. I'm constantly barraged
by requests for the recipe from my out-of-town friends.

P.S. I stole it from Julia Child!

Makes 2 large pancakes (6 to 8 servings)

Batter

    8 extra large eggs
    1 cup unbleached all purpose flour (5 ounces)
    2 tablespoons sugar
    1 teaspoon baking powder
    1/8 teaspoon salt
    2 cups milk
    ¼ cup (½ stick) butter, melted
    2 teaspoons vanilla
    ¼ teaspoon freshly grated nutmeg

Fruit Mixture

    ½ cup (1 stick) unsalted butter
    1-1/3 cups sugar (9½ ounces)
    1 teaspoon cinnamon
    ¼ teaspoon freshly grated nutmeg
    2 large tart apples (Granny Smith or greening), peeled, halved,
      cored and thinly sliced (2 cups)

For batter: Combine first 6 ingredients in mixing bowl and blend with
spoon or electric mixer until smooth. Add melted butter, vanilla,
and nutmeg and blend thoroughly. Let batter stand at room temperature
for 30 minutes, or in refrigerator overnight.

For fruit mixture: Position rack in center of oven and preheat to
425^{0}F. Divide butter evenly and melt in two 10-inch ovenproof skillets,
brushing butter up sides of pan. Remove from heat. Combine sugar,
cinnamon and nutmeg and blend well. Sprinkle 1/3 cup over butter
in each skillet. Divide apple slices and layer evenly over butter.
Sprinkle remaining sugar mixture over apples.

Place skillets over medium-high heat only until mixture bubbles. Divide
batter evenly and gently pour over apples. Transfer skillets to oven
and bake pancakes 15 minutes. Reduce heat to 375^{0}F and bake an additional
10 minutes. Slide onto heated serving platters, cut into wedges
and serve immediately.

A Division of King Broadcasting Company

SEATTLE POLICE DEPARTMENT MEMORANDUM

TO   The Children's Orthopedic Hospital   **DATE** 12/12/85
                        Foundation

FROM   Chief Patrick S. Fitzsimons   **PAGE**   **OF**

SUBJECT Olga's Melt-In-Your-Mouth Pancakes

5 eggs - <u>separated</u>

1 cup sour cream

1 cup cottage cheese

1 cup flour

1 tsp. salt

1/2 tsp baking soda

1 tbs sugar

Sift flour, salt, baking soda and sugar together.

Beat egg yolks well - slowly add sour cream, then cottage
    cheese and blend.

Then blend into flour mixture.

Beat egg whites stiff - fold well into rest of ingredients.

Preheat electric griddle to 400°, then turn back to 350°.

Ladle mixture onto griddle approximately 4-5" in diameter.

Grill until golden brown on one side, then turn until golden
    brown on the other side.

Serve with butter and your favorite syrup.

Serves 4 or 5 people depending on size of appetite.

KIRO Inc.

Broadcast House
Third Avenue & Broad Street
Seattle, Washington 98121
(206) 624-7077

I am delighted and feel honored to be asked to participate in this project.
I hope the cookbook proves to be a great success. The following recipe
was passed down to me from my mother, who made improvements on a recipe she
received from her grandmother. This is a dressing true to Texas-style
cooking, and served with a giblet gravy it is worth every pound you'll gain!

Warmest regards,

Micki Flowers

Ross Ella's Corn Bread Dressing

1 cup of chopped onion (preferably green)
1 cup of chopped celery
1 cup of chopped green pepper
3 cloves of chopped garlic
½ cup of margarine or Wesson oil
4 cups of corn bread crumbs (usually medium-size skillet of corn bread;
 cooked the day before makes tastier dressing)
2 to 4 cups bread crumbs (mix white and brown bread)
1 cup of chopped turkey giblets
1 ¼ cups stock or broth (made from giblets)
1 teaspoon cumin seeds
1 teaspoon sage
1 to 3 teaspoons poultry seasoning
½ teaspoon red pepper (if you like dressing with spicy taste, if not, omit)
2 teaspoons KC or Clabber Girl Baking Powder
1 Tablespoon chopped parsley

pimiento (optional)
small can of green peas (optional)
boiled eggs (optional)

Saute onions, celery, green pepper and garlic in margarine or Wesson oil. Do
not overcook this. Combine with bread crumbs, giblets, and add broth. Toss
lightly with fork, mixing well. Add all seasonings and baking powder, mixing
well but lightly. If you want to add pimiento strips for color, add 1 Tablespoon (cut) to mixture. You can also add a small can of green peas. If mixture
is too dry, add a little more broth to make consistency you want. Add parsley
last and place mixture in a slightly greased casserole dish. Cook about 30
minutes at 350 degrees. Remove from oven and garnish with red pimiento and
green pepper strips, and boiled eggs, if you desire. Make gravy from any leftover broth and giblets, then toss your diet out of the window!

The Bonneville Group

FM Radio: KSEA. Seattle · WRFM. New York · KBIG. Los Angeles · WCLR. Skokie/Chicago · KOIT. San Francisco · KMBR. Kansas City · KAFM. Dallas.
AM Radio: KIRO-AM. Seattle · KBRT. Los Angeles · KMBZ. Kansas City · KSL. Salt Lake City.
Television: KIRO-TV. Seattle · KSL-TV. Salt Lake City

44

John M. Fluke, Jr.
Chairman of the Board
Chief Executive Officer

CINNAMON LOGS

1 1-pound loaf unsliced firm white bread, crusts trimmed
2 cups milk
5 eggs, beaten
2 tablespoon sugar
1/2 to 3/4 teaspoon cinnamon
1/2 teaspoon vanilla

Pinch of grated nutmeg, fresh
Oil for deep frying
Butter and maple

Cut bread into 4x2x2 inch rectangular logs. Let stand to dry slightly.

Blend milk, eggs, sugar, cinnamon, vanilla and nutmeg in medium bowl.
Pour into shallow pan large enough to hold bread in one layer. Arrange
bread in milk mixture, turning to coat all sides. Chill until liquid is
absorbed, several hours or overnight.

Heat oil to 360. Fry logs in batches until golden brown on all sides, about
3 to 4 minutes. Drain on paper towels. Sprinkle with powdered sugar if
desired.

John M. Fluke Jr.

John Fluke Mfg. Co., Inc. / PO Box C9090 / Everett WA 98206 / (206) 347 6100 / TWX 910 445 2943 / TLX 185102

FINE JEWELERS SINCE 1886

PAUL FRIEDLANDER'S PERSONAL SALAD DRESSING
(for two people)

Using a wooden bowl and a wooden muddler,
put one clove of garlic into the bowl and
mash with salt. After completely mashing
the garlic and the salt together, add the
juice of half a lemon. Add to this mixture
one tablespoon of imported vinegar to four
tablespoons of imported olive oil.

Mix thoroughly and serve.......

THEN EAT YOUR WAY TO HEAVEN!!!

2603 THIRD AVENUE   SEATTLE, WASHINGTON 98121   (206) 441-6700

DICK FRIEL'S
MACHO MEAT LOAF

(For A Manly Kind of Meal!)

Once and for all a **real** meat loaf that's mostly beef and full of wonderful meaty flavor. Serve hot with a mild salsa or let cool --- wrap and refrigerate .... guaranteed star of any picnic you put on!

Ingredients:

2 cups minced onions, browned in 2 tablespoons of butter
1 cup fresh white bread crumbs
2 lbs. ground extra lean beef
1 lb. ground pork
1/2 cup dry red wine
1/2 cup beef boullion
2 large eggs
1 cup grated cheddar cheese
1 tablespoon salt
1/2 teaspoon pepper
2 teaspoons each of: Thyme and paprika
1 teaspoon each of: Allspice and oregano
3 bay leaves on top

Mixing:

Squeeze and squish all the ingredients and flavorings together with your bare hands. Now form into a football loaf shape on a buttered baking pan. Top with bay leaves.

Baking:

Bake for about 1½ hours in the middle of your oven at about 350°. You know when the meat loaf is done when a meat thermometer reads 155°. But don't poke it until it's been cooking for at least 1½ hours.

Serving:

Let it cool for 30 minutes --- pour off fat and juices. Transfer to cutting board or serving platter. Serve hot with a great salsa or thick rich tomato sauce. Or wrap it in foil, put in the fridge and make fabulous sandwiches for your next picnic in the San Juans or tailgate party at Husky Stadium.

Serves eight.

6529 Northeast 61st St.   Seattle WA 98115

SEATTLE SUPERSONICS

P.O. Box 900911
Seattle, WA 98109-9711

Oriental Bites

Wrap whole waterchestnuts with 1/3 slice bacon and secure
with pick. Bake on rack at 350° for 25 minutes.

Combine

      1/3 cup soy sauce
      1/3 cup catsup
      1/3 cup brown sugar

Pour over bites and bake another 20-30 minutes.

      Frank Furtado

2006 SO. WELLER STREET
P.O. BOX 24327
SEATTLE, WASHINGTON 98124
Phone: (206) 322-0931

Gai's Seattle French Baking Co., Inc.

We are pleased to submit the following recipe to be used in the
Children's Orthopedic Cookbook.

BISCOTTI BREAD/COOKIE

2½#   Flour
1½#   Granulated Sugar
1/2# Whole Eggs
1/2# Water
2 oz. Salad Oil
5/8 oz., Baking Soda
1/3 oz. Salt
1/2 oz. Lemon Flavor
1/2 oz. Vanilla
1/2# Mixed Fruit
1/2# Raisins
2 oz. Nuts

Mix all liquid ingredients together. Add all dry ingredients and mix
3 minutes. Let rest for 45 to 60 minutes.

Scale into 1# pieces and mold into desired configuration.
Bake 375° for 12 to 15 minutes.

Sincerely,

GAI'S SEATTLE FRENCH BAKING COMPANY INC.

Don Gai
VICE PRESIDENT AND GENERAL MANAGER

Virginia Galle

PASTIES have been a favorite main dish of mine since childhood. During my grade school years, we lived in the Upper Peninsula of Michigan in a community with immigrants from Cornwall, England. Cornish pasties were everywhere-- in bakeries, at the County Fair, at picnics and church suppers.

They were not available in other midwestern cities where we lived, so as a teenager, I experimented and came up with the following recipe. I cannot claim authenticity except as a faithful reproduction of the Pasty I remember. Pasties are now a Galle family tradition, which I am happy to share.

VIRGINIA'S PASTIES

Flour 3 cups
Salt 1/2 teaspoon
Margarine 1 cup
Cold Water 8 tablespoons

Beef round or sirloin 1/2 lb.
                        cubed.
Peel and dice:
  1 Rutabaga
  1/2 cup Potato
  1/2 cup Carrot
  1 medium onion

Salt 1/2 teaspoon
Butter 1/4 cup

Sift flour with salt, cut in margarine, add water, and stir to form a dough. Knead on a floured board until just smooth. Wrap and chill 30 minutes.

Combine remaining ingredients, except butter, and toss until thoroughly blended. Roll dough and cut into four 5-inch circles. Divide beef mixture and place on 1/2 of each circle. Dot with butter. Moisten edges with water and fold other half over beef. Crimp edges firmly together. Bake at 425° for ten minutes, reduce heat to 350° and bake 40 to 45 minutes until golden brown.

Serves 4.

Pasties are hearty, very portable, and heart-warming in cold weather!

Virginia Galle

WASHINGTON WALDORF SALAD

Apples	2, cored and chopped
Celery	1 cup diced
Raisins	1/2 cup
Walnuts	1/3 cup coarsely chopped
Mayonnaise	3/4 cup
Lemon juice	2 tablespoons

Toss together apples, celery, raisins and walnuts;
stir in mixture of mayonnaise and lemon juice.
Serve in a large bowl or on individual, lettuce-
lined plates. Serves 4 to 6.

KRUNCHY DELIGHTS

Cream 1 cup butter with 1 cup sugar.
Add 1 cup flour and dash of salt.
Work in 2 cups of quick oatmeal.

Make into small balls. Put on cookie sheet. Press
very thin with fingers or fork. Bake until very
light golden brown at 400 degrees.

mary gates

Blackberry Cake

Cream 1/2 cup butter and add 1 cup sugar

Add: 2 beaten eggs
     1 tsp soda in 4 T. sour milk
     1 tsp each cinnamon, cloves and nutmeg
     1 3/4 cups flour
Fold in 1 cup small wild blackberries

Icing - Cream 1/4 lb. butter. Add 2 cups powdered sugar, 1 egg and vanilla

Bake in 2 - 9" pans for approx. 25 min. at 350. Do not overbake.

This was a secret recipe of my grandmother's for many years.

LAW OFFICES

DIAMOND & SYLVESTER

10800 N.E.8TH STREET   SUITE 1040

BELLEVUE, WA 98004

(AREA 206) 453-9119

———————

SEATTLE OFFICE
FOURTH FLOOR   HOGE BUILDING
SEATTLE, WASHINGTON 98104
(AREA 206) 623-1330

———————

PLEASE REPLY TO BELLEVUE OFFICE

JOHN N. SYLVESTER
ALBERT O. PRINCE
RICHARD M. FOREMAN
MICHEL P. STERN
CRAIG S. STERNBERG
JOHN T. PETRIE
WILLIAM J. CRUZEN
F. DOUGLAS RUUD
JOHN W. HEMPELMANN
ALAN D. JUDY
JAMES M. THOMAS
TERRY E. THOMSON
LEE KRAFT

———————

GARY D. GAYTON
  OF COUNSEL

JOSEF DIAMOND
COUNSEL TO THE FIRM

SIMON WAMPOLD
ROBERT E. HIBBS
PAUL SIKORA
S. RANDALL JOHNSON
JOHN P. ERLICK
JOSEPH J. STRAUS
JANET A. IRONS
DAVID A. PETERS
MURRAY STAKESBY LEWIS
SARAH WEAVER
DANIEL P. MALLOVE
MARTHA ANAMOSA
MICHAEL B. KING
SHERI L. FLIES
TERRENCE I. DANYSH

KIDNEY STEW

3 or 4 calf kidneys   flour
2 or 3 garlic cloves, chopped   salt
1 medium sized red pepper, chopped   pepper

Slice the calf kidneys crosswise and soak them in cold water for one hour. After soaking, pat kidneys dry. Roll in flour, salt and pepper. Brown kidneys in bacon grease. Remove kidneys from pan and in same pan, brown the garlic cloves. Add red pepper. Add kidneys. Add enough hot water to almost cover ingredients. Simmer slowly for one hour. The mixture will thicken. Serve over rice. Makes 6 servings.

This recipe has been in Gary Gayton's mother's family for 3 generations.

Tim Girvin Design, Inc.   911 Western Avenue   Seattle   206 623 7808
                             Suite 408   WA 98104   206 623 7918

                                                                    Telecopier number
                                                                    206 623 7816

"BAGNA CAUDA"

This is one of our favorite recipes for casual and intimate
gatherings to serve as appetizers or as a light meal prolonged
over conversation. It is a hot anchovy and garlic "dip" with
raw and steamed vegetables and breadsticks.

To serve six:

Prepare and arrange any assortment of vegetables you like -
cucumbers (peeled, seeded and cut into spears) - carrots -
celery - red and green peppers - mushrooms - cherry tomatoes -
cauliflower and broccoli flowerets - radishes - fennel sticks -
scallions - romaine leaves - steamed baby red potatoes, are all
great - along with lots of breadsticks.

2 cups heavy cream
4 tablespoons butter
8 flat anchovy fillets, drained, rinsed and finely chopped
1 teaspoon finely chopped garlic
1 canned white truffle, finely chopped (optional)

In a heavy 1-quart enameled or stainless steel saucepan, bring
the cream to a boil and cook it, stirring frequently, for about
15-20 minutes, or until it has thickened and has reduced to
about 1 cup.

Choose a 3 or 4 cup enameled or flameproof earthenware casserole
that fits over a candle warmer, spirit lamp or electric hot tray.
On the stove, melt the butter in the casserole over low
heat; do not let it brown. Add the anchovies and garlic, then
the reduced cream and serve.

Buon Appetito!

JEAN H. GODDEN
COLUMNIST

OSLO KRINGLE
Coffee Cake

1 cup of water
1 stick of butter or margarine
1 cup of flour
3 eggs
1/2 teaspoon almond flavoring
dash of salt

Place water and butter in sauce pan and bring to
a boil. Remove from the heat and add flour,
stirring until smooth. Add eggs, one at a time,
stirring after each addition. Then add salt and
flavoring.

Spread thin on a large cookie sheet. Bake
at 375 for 15 minutes, then 350 for 10-15
minutes. The kringle should be golden and
slightly puffy.
Remove from the oven and drizzle with
powdered sugar, mixed with warm water and
almond flavoring (another 1/2 teaspoon.)

Cut into squares and serve.

KOMO

Radio and Television

FROM: KATHI GOERTZEN

"IRMA'S CREATION"   (IRMA IS MY MOM)

WHEN YOU'RE IN A HURRY AND EXPECTING 6 FOR DINNER,
MOM SUGGESTED THIS DISH ONE NIGHT AND IT WAS A BIG
HIT WITH MY GUESTS...AND IT'S EASY.

CHOP A CARROT, A PIECE OF CELERY OR TWO AND A SMALL
ONION.
PLACE 6 CHICKEN BREASTS IN A CAKE PAN WITH VEGETABLES.
SEASON WITH SALT, PEPPER, THYME, OR OTHER HERBS.
MIX ONE CUP CHICKEN BROTH WITH ½-1 CUP WHITE WINE.
POUR OVER CHICKEN.
BAKE 40-45 MINUTES (OR UNTIL DONE) AT 350 DEGREES.
YOU MAY WANT TO BROIL FOR A MINUTE OR TWO TO BROWN.
PLACE MEAT ON PLATTER FOR SERVING.
POUR SAUCE IN FRYING PAN AND BOIL DOWN JUST BEFORE
SERVING.
SPREAD THICKENED SAUCE OVER CHICKEN BREASTS AND SERVE!

Kathi Goertzen
KOMO 4 News

100 Fourth Avenue North, Seattle, Washington 98109 (206) 443-4000
Fisher Broadcasting Inc. • ABC Affiliates.

SLADE GORTON
WASHINGTON

COMMITTEES:
COMMERCE, SCIENCE, AND
TRANSPORTATION
BANKING, HOUSING, AND
URBAN AFFAIRS
BUDGET
SMALL BUSINESS
INDIAN AFFAIRS

513 HART SENATE OFFICE BUILDING
(202) 224-2621

2988 JACKSON FEDERAL BUILDING
915 SECOND AVENUE
SEATTLE, WA 98174
(206) 442-5545

770 U.S. COURT HOUSE
W. 920 RIVERSIDE AVENUE
SPOKANE, WA 99201
(509) 456-6816

FIRST FEDERAL PLAZA, SUITE 445
1220 MAIN STREET
VANCOUVER, WA 98660
(206) 696-7838

United States Senate
WASHINGTON, DC 20510

A Favorite Recipe from Sally Gorton

Overnight Layered Green Salad

1 Medium head iceberg lettuce
1 bunch green onions
1 8 oz. can water chestnuts
1/2 red or green pepper, seeded
2 stalks celery
1 package (10 oz.) frozen green peas,
   slightly thawed and separated
2 cups mayonnaise
2 teaspoons sugar
1/2 cup Parmesan cheese
1 teaspoon salt
1/4 teaspoon garlic powder
3/4 pound crisp-fried bacon, crumbles
3 hard boiled eggs
2 tomatoes

If possible, use slicing disc with food
processor to slice lettuce, chestnuts,
peppers and celery. Cut onions with
sharp knife.

In glass bowl, layer lettuce, water
chestnuts, peppers, celery, onions and
green peas.

Mix mayonnaise, sugar, cheese, salt and
garlic powder together and pour over top
of layered ingredients.

Before serving, sprinkle crumbled bacon
over the top and decorate with eggs slices
and tomato wedges.

Serve with tongs or spoon and fork to dig
deeply.

Makes 8 to 10 generous servings.

LOIS GRAHAM
9210 N.E. 25th Street
Bellevue, WA 98004
206/454-3299

SWEDISH PEPPARKAKOR

4 cups sifted flour
1 t baking soda
1 t ground nutmeg
1½ t ground ginger
3/4 t ground cloves
1 cup butter
1 cup sugar
1/3 cup dark molasses (or unsulfured)
1/2 cup cream

Cream together butter and sugar. Beat in molasses. Alternately add the combined dry ingredients and cream. The last cup of flour requires hand-kneading. Add more flour if necessary. Knead and roll with hands on floured board. Form into four patties, wrap each in waxed paper and chill at least two hours or overnight.

When ready to bake, remove one patty at a time, work with hands until very pliable, and carefully roll out on floured pastry cloth to 1/16" thickness. Cut with favorite cookie cutters, transfer to baking sheet (covered with parchment paper works well) and decorate with colored sugars.

Bake in pre-heated 350° oven until cookies begin to brown on the edges. Remove to cool on a flat surface. When cool, pack carefully in airtight tins with paper between layers. Cookies will keep for a month.

My grandmother brought this family recipe from her home in Sweden when she immigrated to America as a young woman in 1889. Decorating the pepparkakor in elaborate and inventive designs is a family tradition which begins the Christmas season.

Lois Graham's typically large, color-filled paintings are non-objective, all over networks of marks; paintings "about paint" and the build up of oil pigment. Her paint is laid on in lush, juicy, rich surfaces which scatter light and keep the eye moving across a spectrum of color.

This is a dry barbeque sprinkle that is not for the faint
hearted. But, if you like it "hot and zesty" you'll
love it. I have used it on steaks, ribs, chops and chicken.

Norm's Hot Barbeque Sprinkle

        2 heaping tablespoons of black pepper

        6 heaping tablespoons of salt

        3 heaping tablespoons of garlic powder

        1 heaping tablespoon of cayenne

        3 heaping tablespoons of chili powder

        4 heaping tablespoons of paprika

Mix ingredients in a bowl.   You can then either:
1) sprinkle on meat; or 2) put mixture in a paper bag
with meat and shake numerous times to coat meat thoroughly.
This mix serves as a crust; sealing in the juices.
Save leftover mix for future use.

Enjoy.......

Norm Gregory

Norm Gregory
KOMO Afternoons, 3 - 7 pm.

100 Fourth Avenue North, Seattle, Washington 98109 (206) 223-4000
Fisher Broadcasting Inc. • ABC Affiliates.

BOARD OF TRUSTEES
Mrs. Gilbert W. Anderson
   Chairman
Mrs. Fredrick E. Cockrill
   President

Mrs. Michael Albrecht
Mrs. Prudence Baldwin
Mrs. Milton H. Bohart
Mrs. Richard B. Brannon
Mrs. Philip L. Burton
Mrs. Peter W. Eising
Mrs. Richard E. Friel
Mrs. William H. Gates
Mrs. Arnold H. Groth
Mrs. Robert J. Habegger
Mrs. William P. Hagen
Mrs. Gerald E. Heron
Mrs. Jerome M. Johnson
Mrs. Minor Lile, Jr.
Mrs. Bruce Maines
Mrs. Jeremy Mattox
Mrs. Stanley N. Minor
Mrs. Charles S. Mullen
Mrs. MacMillan Pringle
Mrs. John W. Reynolds
Mrs. Herman Sarkowsky
Mrs. James R. Scott
Mrs. Stuart M. Sloan
Mrs. James M. Smith
Mrs. Pat Stusser
Mrs. Holt W. Webster
Mrs. John Wells

**HONORARY
BOARD OF TRUSTEES**
Mrs. William M. Allen
Mrs. Clarence Ambrose, Jr.
Mrs. Philip W. Bailey
Mrs. Emery P. Bayley
Mrs. Robert J. Behnke
Mrs. John D. Bixby
Mrs. William D. Bowden
Mrs. A. Scott Bullitt
Mrs. Wetherill Collins
Mrs. Ward M. Doland
Mrs. Stuart C. Frazier
Mrs. Dickinson C. Harper
Mrs. John H. Hauberg
Mrs. Paul N. Howard
Mrs. Charles T. Jordan
Mrs. B. Letcher Lambuth
Mrs. J. Richard Lane
Mrs. Burns Lindsey
Mrs. J. Collins Lloyd
Mrs. Richards L. Loesch
Mrs. Beale McCulloch
Mrs. Henry B. Owen
Mrs. George V. Powell
Mrs. William G. Reed
Mrs. John E. Ryan, Jr.
Mrs. Morton L. Schwabacher
Mrs. William L. Trudgian
Mrs. Claude E. Wakefield
Mrs. Charles K. Wiggins

ADMINISTRATION
Treuman Katz
   Chief Executive Officer

GRANDMA'S BEST EVER OATMEAL COOKIES

1 cup of raisins, cooked 20 minutes in enough water to have
    5 teaspoons of water left.

1/2 cup butter
1/2 cup lard } cream together with 1 cup of sugar.

2 eggs, beaten, added to above
1 teaspoon baking soda, dissolved in 5 teaspoons of raisin water
2 cups of quick oatmeal
2 cups of flour
Dash of salt
1 teaspoon of vanilla
1/2 teaspoon cinnamon
Dash of freshly grated nutmeg (or 1/4 tsp. ground nutmeg)
Drain raisins and add
1 cup of coarsely chopped nuts (either pecans or walnuts).

Cook raisins for 20 minutes, covered, with enough water
to have 5 teaspoons of water left.

Cream together butter and lard with 1 cup of sugar, then
add the slightly beaten eggs. Dissolve the baking soda in
the 5 teaspoons of raisin water and add along with the
vanilla.

Stir in the oatmeal, flour and the dash of salt, the
cinnamon and the nutmeg.

Fold in the drained raisins and the chopped nuts.

Drop rounded teaspoons full on a slightly greased baking
sheet and bake at 375° for 10-12 minutes.

Peggy Habegger
Peggy Habegger
COHMC Board of Trustees

Anne Hallett
1502 E. Olin Place
Seattle, WA 98112

Steak Sandwich with Walla Walla Sweets

Marinade:	2/3	cup	beer
	1/3	cup	cooking oil
	1	teaspoon	salt
	1/4	teaspoon	garlic powder
	1/4	teaspoon	pepper

Topping #1:	2	tablespoons	butter
	1/2	teaspoon	paprika
	4	cups	Walla Walla sweet onions

Topping # 2:	1	cup	sour cream, warmed
	1/2	teaspoon	prepared horseradish

12 slices sour dough French bread, toasted
2-pound flank steak

Combine beer, oil, salt, garlic powder and pepper in a shallow dish. Place flank steak in the marinade and cover. Marinate several hours at room temperature, turning several times. Drain. Broil flank steak 5-7 minutes per side. Slice very thin on the diagonal.

Meanwhile, chop two or three Walla Walla sweet onions (or regular yellow onions if the Walla Walla champs aren't in season). In a skillet, melt the butter and add onions. Cook at low temperature until they are tender, but not browned.

Put the sour cream in a saucepan, add the horseradish, and warm.
Toast the sour dough bread and butter lightly.

To serve, arrange steak slices on the sour dough. Top with onions and then with the sour cream/horseradish. Serves 6.

I stole this recipe, long a family favorite, out of a magazine in my doctor's office after having waited for him for an hour. No big deal (the next time I simply got up and left, telling his nurse to have him call me when he had time to see me), but it has remained for me a fond memory of a first tiny protest against insensitivity.

KOMO
Radio and Television

My son is now a strapping, six-foot-five
seventeen year old.

But, I can remember when Steve was just
a little guy and had to have an ear
operation. I will always remember the
skill of the surgeon and the fine care
he received at Children's Orthopedic.

Best of luck with the SEATTLE'S CELEBRITY
CHEFS cookbook.

Happy to take part.

Sincerely,

Jim Harriott
Managing Editor

JIM HARRIOTT'S TARRAGON CHICKEN

½ pound large, fresh mushrooms (from Pike Place Market, if possible) or 8 ounce can of sliced mushrooms (if not)

4 chicken breasts boned and skinned (about 1 pound, Washington grown)

1 cup white wine (after appropriate research at Chateau Ste. Michelle)

2 tablespoons butter (if being careful of diet, margarine will do)

½ teaspoon tarragon (the "magic" ingredient)

½ teaspoon salt

1 tablespoon white flour (Does the name Fisher come to mind?)

Wash and slice the mushrooms (if using canned mushrooms be sure to drain off liquid).

Melt 2 tablespoons butter (or margarine) in large, heavy skillet.

Sauté chicken until brown on both sides.

Add mushrooms. Sauté 1 minute.

Add 3/4 cup white wine, tarragon and salt. Reduce heat.

Simmer for 15 minutes or until tender.

Remove chicken breasts and place on warm platter.

Stir 1 tablespoon white flour into ¼ cup wine until well combined.

Stir into wine and mushroom mixture.

Pour mixture over chicken.

Serve and enjoy!

THE
PETRA
CORPORATION

I am enclosing my favorite recipe. This has been special in the Harshman household for forty years. My wife Dorothy's Grandmother brought it from Sweden almost one hundred years ago. I used to ask her how do you make these Swedish Pancakes and she would always reply, a little flour a little this and little that and beat them till they have the right feel. Finally after many inquiries I convinced her to write it down. So here is Swedish Pancakes:

> 2 Cups Flour
> 3 Cups Milk
> 1 Tablespoon Sugar
> Pinch of Salt

Blend this together with hand or electric beater until smooth.

Add: Five eggs - beat together until smooth

> (quite thin)

Bake on a hot griddle 400 - 450
Pancakes may be rolled Swedish style a la crepe, filled with fresh fruit or preserves or they may be stacked like conventional pancakes with syrup or jam.

This recipe will serve a family of five. My personal feeling is if you mix batter the night before and then beat lightly just before baking they are better. Enjoy!

Marv Harshman
Marv Harshman

1756 114TH AVENUE S.E., SUITE 234, BELLEVUE, WASHINGTON 98004 PHONE (206) 455-1157

KIRO Inc.

Broadcast House
2807 Third Avenue
P.O. Box C21326
Seattle, WA 98111-7077
(206) 382-5200

Kenneth L. Hatch
President/Chief Executive Officer

HOT BEEF, COOL WATERCRESS SALAD

For this hot-and-cold salad, you stir-fry seasoned beef and place it on a bed of cool watercress. The hot soy-flavored beef slightly wilts the raw nippy greens and sweet-tart onions. Serve as a light lunch entree with rice.

Have all ingredients prepared before you start cooking the meat.

Hot Beef and Watercress Salad

1/2 pound lean boneless beefsteak, such as sirloin or fillet,
    about 1 inch thick
4   cloves garlic, minced or pressed
2   teaspoons soy sauce
1   teaspoon sugar
2   tablespoons salad oil
2   tablespoons white wine vinegar
1/4 teaspoon pepper
1   small white onion, thinly sliced (about 1/2 pound watercress)

Trim off and discard excess fat from meat. Cut meat into 1/8-inch thick slices about 3 inches long. In a small bowl, mix beef with garlic, soy, 1/2 teaspoon of the sugar, and 1 teaspoon of the oil. Cover and chill at least 30 minutes or up to overnight.

In a separate bowl, stir together remaining sugar, 2 teaspoons oil, vinegar, and pepper; stir in onion. Cover and chill at least 30 minutes or up to overnight.

Wash watercress; remove and discard thick tough stems. Lightly pack enough of the tender sprigs into a measuring cup to measure 3 cups. Lightly mix watercress with onion in marinade and place on a serving platter.

Place a wok or 10- to 12-inch frying pan over high heat. When pan is hot, add remaining oil and beef. Stir-fry until beef is lightly browned, about 2 minutes. Place over watercress. Makes 2 servings.

- Kenneth L. Hatch
President/CEO
KIRO, Inc.

The Bonneville Group

FM Radio: KSEA, Seattle · WRFM, New York · KBIG, Los Angeles · WCLR, Skokie/Chicago · KOIT, San Francisco · KMBR, Kansas City · KAFM, Dallas.
AM Radio: KIRO-AM, Seattle · KAAM, Dallas · KMBZ, Kansas City · KSL, Salt Lake City.
Television: KIRO-TV, Seattle · KSL-TV, Salt Lake City.

SEATTLE SUPERSONICS

P.O. Box 900911
Seattle, WA 98109-9711

BAR-B-QUE SPARE RIBS

1lb. country style spare ribs
½ stick melted butter
½ cup ketchup
1 cup vinegar
1 T. hot sauce
2 cups Kraft B-B-que sauce

Wash ribs and season with salt,pepper and meat tenderizer.
Cover and refrigerate overnight.

Put in pot and cover with water. Boil. Lower heat to
medium and cook about 1 hour. Remove ribs from pot and
place in baking dish.

Mix sauce all together and pour over ribs. Bake at 350
(covered) for about 40 minutes or when meat begins to
peel away from the bone.

Gerald and Marie Henderson

King County Executive
Tim Hill

SWEDISH MEATBALLS

Serves 6

Meatballs:
1½ lbs. ground chuck
½ C sour cream
¼ C bread crumbs
2 t salt
¼t pepper
½t garlic powder
1/8t thyme
1 T minced onion
1½t Accent
1 T butter

Gravy:
1 C sour cream
¼t garlic powder
½t sugar
1t dried dill
2T lemon juice

Mix well all meatball ingredients. Mixture
should be soft but hold shape. Shape into 35
small balls. Place on tray. Chill 15 minutes.
Heat butter in large skillet until sizzling.
Brown meatballs quickly. Pour off extra fat.
Put meatballs in 275 degree oven for 10 minutes.
Add 1 C sour cream in skillet. Put in gravy
seasonings and stir until just bubbly. Pour
any juices from baking pan into skillet and
blend in. Serve meatballs topped with gravy
and garnish with paprika and parsley.

Tim Hill
King County Executive

400 King County Courthouse 516 Third Avenue Seattle, Washington 98104 (206) 344-4040

The Seattle Times

FAIRVIEW AVENUE NORTH AND JOHN STREET
POST OFFICE BOX 70
SEATTLE, WASHINGTON 98111

JOHN HINTERBERGER'S CLAMMED SPAGHETTI

This recipe for a pedestrian (but wonderful) dish of pasta first appeared in The Times almost 13 years ago. Requests for copies have come in steadily ever since. Originally conceived of as a "poor student supper for six," it has remained a family favorite long after economics dictated its frequent application. Slightly warmed over (or even cold), it is a devastating breakfast.

To feed six (four really big eaters, or three gluttons):

Put a half cup of olive oil in a large black cast-iron skillet. Heat the oil slowly and add one dried red chili pepper which you have chopped up. Avoid getting any pepper oils into your eyes.

Chop one great big onion or two not-so-big onions and add to the oil. Mash three big garlic cloves and stir them in. Cook slowly for a long time. You want the onions to break down gradually without browning. This can take as long as half an hour.

While it is bubbling lightly, throw in a generous bunch of sweet basil, fresh, if possible, dried, if not. Sprinkle a tablespoon of oregano over the onions. Salt and pepper to taste. Use freshly ground black pepper. Now open two cans of chopped clams (buy chopped clams instead of minced; they are larger pieces and give you something to chew on).

Drain the cans but save the liquid. Pour the clam broth into the onions after they have cooked for about half an hour. Increase the heat a little and bring the broth to a simmer. Let it cook down for a while until it once again is somewhat oily, instead of watery. Keep it hot until you are ready to eat. Notice that you have not added the clams (You have? Tough. And they will be).

Heat water for the spaghetti. Use a lot of it. Throw in a tablespoon of salt and another tablespoon of oil. Cook the spaghetti at as full a boil as you can without having the whole mess boil over. Don't overcook it; most Americans do. Spaghetti should not be soft; it should be tender but offer some resistance to the tooth.

Five minutes before the pasta is done, add the drained clams and a half cup of chopped parsley to the sauce. Also add three tablespoons of freshly grated cheese--romano or parmesan.

Simmer the clams five minutes at low heat. Any longer and they get tough. If you are feeling fancy, add some small canned (or uncanned) precooked shrimp. If you had a couple of mushrooms, you could have sauteed them and added them to the sauce. A couple of chunks of pimento adds color.

Now, a crucial step. After you have drained the spaghetti--a pound for six, by the way--slop it back into the large skillet in which you are heating the sauce. Do not ever rinse cooked pasta.

Carefully toss the spaghetti in the skillet while it is still over the low heat. This is important. It restores the certain firmness to the pasta, coats each strand with the oily sauce, and drives off a little water. Do this about three minutes.

Slather plenty of grated cheese over the top and serve from the black skillet. A green salad goes well with it; a cheap white jug wine tops it off.

Best regards,

John Hinterberger

John Hinterberger

HOLDEN PACIFIC
INCORPORATED.

FRAGRANT PUMPKIN BISQUE
Serves 6 - 8

This rich and creamy bisque will surprise your family and impress your guests. They won't believe how easy it is to fix--ten minutes at the outside. Garnish with green onions for a hearty winter soup, or serve chilled with fresh herbs for a refreshing first course in summer.

THE CREAM MIXTURE:

Make this first so that the sour cream and yoghurt develop the lovely, slightly acidic taste one finds in French creme fraiche.

1 cup sour cream
1 cup plain yoghurt
about ½ cup half and half or whipping cream
1 TB sugar

Combine the sour cream and the yoghurt. Slowly add the half & half or whipping cream and whisk gently until the mixture has the consistency of heavy cream. Sweeten with 1 TB sugar. Set aside.

THE PUMPKIN SOUP BASE

Homemade chicken stock tastes best, but condensed broth works well. The onions (and carrot) add natural sweetness.

2 TB butter
¼ cup finely chopped onion
2 TB finely grated carrot (optional)
3 cups homemade chicken stock (or 2 10-½ oz. cans condensed chicken broth)
1 29-oz. can pumpkin (about 3 cups)
salt
white pepper
dill

Saute the finely chopped onion (and the optional grated carrot), in butter until soft but not brown. Add the chicken stock or condensed chicken broth and simmer briefly.

Stir in the pumpkin and heat through. Add 1 tsp salt (or to taste), ¼ tsp pepper, and about ¼ tsp dill. Mixture will be quite thick at this point.

FINAL PREPARATION

Look in your kitchen and garden for green and crunchy things. For example, depending on availability and season, you might use some combination of:

2 fresh green onions
2 TB fresh chives
2 TB chopped parsley
2 TB chopped fresh spinach

Off heat, fold the cream mixture into the pumpkin soup. Heat, but do not let the soup reach a boil. Stir in the fresh onions or herbs.

For hot bisque, ladle into soup bowls. Put a dollop of sour cream in the middle of each portion, garnish with a sprinkle of dill, green onions, parsley, or chives, and serve at once.

Fold cold soup, chill. Thin with cream before serving, if desired, and garnish with sour cream and herbs.

HHH **Harley H. Hoppe**

The Children's Orthopedic Hospital and Medical
Center has made a contribution beyond descrip-
tion to the quality of life we enjoy in the
Seattle area.

I am pleased to participate in this worthy
endeavor.

Sincerely,

Harley H. Hoppe

SEATTLE SOLE

1 - 2 eggs

1 Tbsp. finely chopped parsley

1 tsp. dill weed

4 sole fillets (approximately 3½ ounces each)

1 tsp. salt

3 Tbsp. oil

3 Tbsp. butter (melted with 1 Tbsp. of lemon)

Beat eggs, parsley and dillweed until foamy.

Dip each fillet in egg mixture.

Place in pan that has oil in it on high heat until lightly browned.

Place fillets in shallow baking pan.

Drizzle lemon butter and bake in 375° oven for 5 minutes.

Garnish with lemon.

PAUL HORIUCHI
9773 ARROWSMITH SOUTH
SEATTLE, WASHINGTON 98118

Meat and Vegetable Dish
*****

1 # sukiyaki beef strips

½ Nappa (Chinese Cabbage)

2 or 3 green peppers -cut lengthwise into 1 " strips

1 # mushrooms - Cut in half

2 bunches green onions, including white part

1 large dry onion - sliced

Any vegetables may be used as you prefer.

Vegetable oil,

Prepared teriyaki sauce (Commercial)

Arrange vegetables on a large platter.

Put oil in electric frying pan , when heated
place beef, and vegetables and cook until each individual
feels it is cooked to their liking.

This is all done at the table after everyone is seated.

Each one serves himself from the skillet. Dip the pieces
into the teriyaki sauce served individually in a small
bowl.

Serve with rice. Serves about 4 people.

Paul Horiuchi

74

BERGMAN LUGGAGE CO., INC.
1930 3rd Avenue
SEATTLE, WASHINGTON 98101

Recipe from JAY HURWITZ

Beef and Vegetable Stir-Fry

Vegetables:

    4 carrots chopped
    2 small onions chopped
    6 oz. mushrooms sliced
    1 cup broccoli (chopped into bite-size pieces)
    1/2 cup sliced waterchestnuts
    1 red pepper chopped (green if preferred)
    1/4 cup sliced almonds (optional)

Meat:

    1-1/4 lbs. of beef tenderloin or sirloin, thinly sliced

Sauce ingredients (pre-mix):

    3/4 cup beef broth
    1/2 cup soy sauce
    1/4 cup sherry
    3 tablespoons sugar (optional)

Heat electric wok (or skillet) to 400 degrees. Heat 2 tablespoons of
peanut oil, in wok. Add vegetables and brown them only. Their full cooking
time will be done later. Remove all vegetables and set aside while cooking
the meat. Quickly brown the meat, push to one side, add the browned vegetables and half the sauce, cook until vegetables are crisp/tender; add the
other half or sauce and thicken with corn starch (stir in 1 teaspoonful at
a time until it reaches the thickness and consistency desired). Can be
served as is, or over rice or noodles. Yields 4 servings.

UNIVERSITY OF WASHINGTON
SEATTLE, WASHINGTON 98195

Tom D. Ivey, M.D.
Associate Professor
Chief, Division of Cardiothoracic Surgery
Department of Surgery, RF—25

SALMON SALAD ON PASTRY

This recipe uses either eclair shells or toasted, scooped out brioches to hold a delightful, light salmon-cucumber filling, topped with hollandaise sauce. Served with a tossed salad and a good Chardonnay it's a delightful lunch or light dinner.

6	Eclair shells or brioches
1 Can	Sockeye salmon or 2 baked salmon steaks
2 Cups	Sour half and half
1 Cup	Seeded, chopped cucumber
1 Tblsp	Chopped shallot
1/8 Tsp	Dill weed
	Dash of lemon juice

Mix crumbled salmon with cucumber, shallot, dill and lemon juice. If using brioches, cut off tops and hollow out. Toast lightly on the oven grill setting just before serving. Fill with either cold or warmed salmon mixture. Place top of pastry over the salad. Top with a dollop of hollandaise sauce.

Pursuing salmon on the open ocean or open buffet is one of the Ivey Family's favorite activities!

Telephone: (206) 543-3093

Enclosed are two of Coach Don James' favorite things to eat!!

Make Ahead Caesar Salad

1 crushed garlic bud
½ teaspoon salt
¼ teaspoon pepper
½ teaspoon dry mustard
1 Tablespoon lemon juice
¼ cup oil
2-3 Tablespoons grated parmesan cheese

Mix in bottom of wooden salad bowl. On top, put cut up lettuce.
DO NOT TOSS. Cover and let stand several hours. Add tomato
wedges and toss. Serve immediately.

- -

My Favorite - Carol's Pecan Pie

3 eggs
1 cup brown sugar
BEAT TILL THICK

ADD:
1 cup light corn syrup
1 cup pecan pieces
1 teaspoon vanilla

PUT IN UNBAKED PIE SHELL

Bake:
300 degrees for 1-1½ hours. Makes 1 nine inch pie.

Pie Crust

2 cups flour
3/4 teaspoon salt
3/4 cup shortening
5 Tablespoons buttermilk (¼cup)

Mix well. Roll out between wax paper. Put in pie pan.

Thousand Trails, Inc.

15325 S.E. 30th Place
Bellevue, Washington 98007
(206) 644-1100

In response to your request, I am delighted to enclose the world's greatest recipe 😊 for huevos rancheros ala Jensen, and my famous Orange Julius drink as inherited from brother Joe Clark. Happy to help.

Huevos Rancheros

1. Deep fry corn tortillas until browned.
2. Generously spread heated refried beans on one side of the tortilla. (When heating the refried beans, season heavily with pepper and some salt to eliminate the naturally bland taste.)
3. Cover refried beans with Ortega Chili Salsa Verde (you can use generously as this salsa is mild).
4. Place one fried egg (sunny side up) on top of the tortilla, beans and salsa.
5. Generously sprinkle shredded cheddar and/or Monterey jack cheese on top. The combination of both cheeses is delightful.
6. Place on cookie sheet and put in oven under broiler until cheese is thoroughly melted. Serve immediately.

Orange Julius

Fill blender one-half full of ice cubes. Add 1 small can frozen orange juice concentrate, 1-1/2 cans vodka, 1/2 can half and half, and one raw egg. Blend and serve. Top with grated nutmeg for an extra frill and thrill.

Enjoy!

Jim Jensen

Norm and Lori Johnson's Chili

This chili was originally created when we were trying to figure out what to do with the 200 tomatoes in our garden that ripened at the same time. One day Lori went out, picked a bunch of them, threw them in a large pot and started adding everything she could find in the refrigerator. She was able to use up lots of the tomatoes, clean out the fridge, and create the best chili I've ever had all in one shot!

This is an easy recipe fo follow because you really can't ruin it by adding a little more "this" or a little less "that." You can create your own "garden fresh" chili by using fresh tomatoes, green peppers, and jalepenos, or substitute canned. Adjust to satisfy your own taste buds and ENJOY!

2 cans whole tomatoes (28 oz. each)
1 can tomato paste (12 oz.)
1/3 cup Louisiana hot sauce (or tabasco)
1/3 cup worcestershire sauce
1/4 cup ketchup
2 Tbs. chili powder
1 Tbs. cayenne pepper
1/2 tsp. garlic powder
1 tsp. coarse ground pepper

1 tsp. cumin
5 cans dark red kidney beans
  drained (15¼ oz. each)
1½ lb. ground beef (lean preferred)
1/4 cup tequila

Finely chop the following and saute in large skillet with 2 Tbs. butter or margarine and 1 cup red wine:

2 each- green bell peppers   onions
       red bell peppers   mushrooms
       fresh jalepenos

add to chili, let simmer several hours or all day if possible, stirring occasionally.

For vegetarians: Substitute meat with one more can of kidney beans and more veggies.
Optional: Tequila-it does make the chili a bit more interesting. I have heard beer is good also.
Jalepenos- These definitely make the chili HOT, so if you're not into 5 alarm chili, I suggest you omit the jalepenos.

NORM & LORI JOHNSON

Seattle Seahawks

5305 LAKE WASHINGTON BLVD • KIRKLAND, WA. 98033 • (206) 827-9777

GENE JUAREZ SALONS

What a wonderful surprise to be acknowledged as one of
Seattle's noteworthy personalities. And even more ex-
citing - to be asked to contribute one of my favorite
recipes to your "Seattle's Celebrity Chefs" cookbook!

Enclosed is the recipe I am submitting for your book.
It was chosen because of its regional flair and Seattle's
bounty of fresh food.

I think your idea of a cookbook is great and I truly
hope the proceeds reap a large financial benefit for
Children's Orthopedic Hospital.

Best regards.

Gene

GENE JUAREZ
President

GENE JUAREZ SALONS

SALMON STEAKS IN THREE MUSTARD SAUCE

4 Tbs.	Butter
4	Salmon Steaks, one-inch thick
4 Tbs.	White Wine Vinegar (or tarragon-flavored vinegar)
2 Tbs.	Dijon Mustard
2 Tbs.	Coarse German-Style Mustard
2 tsp.	Dry Mustard
1-1/2 cups	Heavy Cream
	Freshly ground pepper and salt to taste

Melt butter in large skillet and saute salmon over low to medium heat about 5 minutes. Turn and cook 5 more minutes. Set Salmon aside. Add vinegar to skillet, increase heat to medium and cook, scraping up salmon bits, until slightly reduced. Whisk in mustards, blending well. Add cream, reduce heat and blend well. Heat through but DO NOT BOIL. Return salmon to skillet and heat through (2-3 minutes).

SERVES FOUR

Corporate Office
1661 East Olive Way
Seattle, Washington 98102
206/323-7773

Gene Juarez of Bellevue
103 Bellevue Square
Bellevue, Washington 98004
455-5511

Gene Juarez at Four Seasons
Four Seasons Olympic Hotel
411 University
Seattle, Washington 98101
628-0011

Gene Juarez at Nordstrom
1501 5th Avenue
Seattle, Washington 98101
628-1405

Advanced Training Center
1601 Sixth Avenue
Seattle, Washington 98101
622-6611

NEAPOLITAN SEAFOOD CIOPPINO

Four to six servings

PONCHO

PATRONS OF NORTHWEST
CIVIC, CULTURAL AND
CHARITABLE ORGANIZATIONS

OFFICERS 1985-86
Dr. Solomon Katz, President
Michael J. Malone, First Vice President
Patrick McFarlan, Vice President
Mrs. David L. Fluke, Vice President
Mrs. Chester W. Woodside, Vice President
George Akers, Secretary
John Fluke, Jr., Treasurer

BOARD OF TRUSTEES
Michael D. Alhadeff
Margery Aronson
Mrs. Robert H. Baugh
Mrs. Robert S. Beaupre
Carl G. Behnke
Kenneth V. Bellamy
Larry Blake
Robert Blethen
Mrs. Leland Burnett
Mrs. William Champion
Jan E. Clotfelter
Molly Coleman
Mrs. Richard Connelly
Mrs. James C. Coons
James M. Costello
Mrs. H. Tee Crick
Robert V. Dahl
Henry W. Dean
David de Varona
Mrs. Robert B. Dootson
Pat Fearey
Charles Ferraro
Graham Fitch
Mrs. Paul S. Friedlander
Gary Gayton
Peggy L. Golberg
Mrs. David Heerensperger
Mrs. Frederick S. Hoedemaker
Ann Kalberg
James E. Kessi
Gerald R. Kingen
William R. Kopp
G. Chris Kosmos
Edwin C. Laird
Mrs. Donald McAusland
Bruce R. McCaw
James Murphy
Theodore R. Pappas
Mimi V. W. Pierce
Mrs. Stuart Prestrud
Ted Rand
Mrs. William Sanborn
Walter Schoenfeld
John Schwartz
Michael Seller
Sam J. Sherer
Kenneth W. Smith III
Mrs. Richard Soderstrom
Mrs. David Sprague
Mrs. S. W. Thurston
Jean Viereck
Mrs. Robert Denny Watt
Thomas T. Wilson
Mrs. Howard S. Wright
Mrs. David C. Wyman
Hal Wyman

LIFETIME TRUSTEES
Morris J. Alhadeff
Robert M. Arnold
Robert J. Behnke
David S. Bingham
George Briggs
Mrs. John B. Clayburgh
Robert B. Dootson
David A. Ederer
Mrs. Doyle Fowler
David Friedenberg
Paul S. Friedlander
Richard E. Friel
Mrs. Frank Hopkins
Frank Hopkins
C. David Hughbanks
Dillis W. Knapp
Howard Leendertsen
Llewelyn G. Pritchard
Edward A. Rauscher
Faye Sarkowsky
Herman Sarkowsky
Leland C. Shepardson
Mrs. David E. Skinner
James L. Wilson, M.D.
Barbara Rauscher Wise
Bagley Wright
David C. Wyman

ADMINISTRATION
Judith A. Whetzel, Executive Director
Jean B. Robins, Administrative Assistant

1906 - 42nd Avenue East
Seattle, Washington 98112
Telephone 322-3440

1-2 T. olive or vegetable oil
1 large onion, chopped; 1-2 cloves garlic, minced or pressed
1 green pepper, seeded & chopped
1-2 carrots, cut into thin strips
1-2 celery stalks, diced
1/3 cup chopped parsley
1 can (16 oz.) peeled and chopped tomatoes
1-2 cans (8 oz. each) tomato sauce
1 1/2 cups dry white wine
1 tsp. salt or to taste
2 bay leaves
1/2 tsp. each: crushed dried basil, thyme, marjoram, basil
1/2 tsp. dried chili pepper flakes or hot pepper sauce
1 lb. halibut steaks, or other firm whitefish, cut into one-inch cubes
1 dozen fresh clams or mussels in the shell, well scrubbed
1/2 to 1 lb. raw medium shrimp or prawns, shelled and deveined.

1. Heat the oil in a large skillet over medium-high heat. Add onion,
   green pepper, carrot, and garlic and sauté, stirring occasionally,
   until soft, about 5 minutes.
2. Transfer to a large pot with tight-fitting cover. Add tomatoes,
   tomato sauce, bay leaves, salt, basil, marjoram, thyme, and chili
   flakes or hot pepper sauce. Simmer, covered, over medium-low heat
   45 minutes, stirring occasionally.
3. Add the wine; cook uncovered for 10 minutes.
4. Add the celery, halibut, and clams or mussels; simmer, covered,
   5 minutes or until the fish is cooked and the clams are open.
   Discard any clams that did not open during cooking.
5. Add the shrimp and parsley and cook, covered, 3 minutes, or until
   shrimp turn pink.
6. Serve in large soup bowls with hot sourdough bread or rolls.

In my pre-World War II years in Seattle, age had not yet withered
nor custom staled the infinite variety of "ethnic" restaurants. De-
spite the wealth of available seafood here, I cannot recall eating
anything like a genuine cioppino at the prehistoric Ivar's (Keep Clam!)
or the Italian Village Cafe/Restaurant or Gasparetti's (if that
famous eatery was already in existence in those halcyon days).

It was, therefore, only when the 416th Night Fighter Squadron
which I served as Combat Intelligence Officer arrived in Naples, Italy
in September 1943 that I learned to savor and to favor that marvelous
Neapolitan seafood cioppino which I personally hold in far higher re-
gard than Naples' other gifts to civilization: the pizza and three-
stripe ice cream. Indeed, so highly did I esteem cioppino that I
persuaded our Mess Sergeant, the redoubtable Sergeant Sipple, to replace on occasion his favorite Spam, Vienna sausages ("Cap'n, them
thar Vi-eeners, they sho' make a tasty dish"), or chipped beef on
toast ("S.O.S.", in the x-rated version) by cioppino improvised by a
fugitive from a Mississippi or Louisiana bayou.

I hope the above recipe works by you. Enjoy!

Solomon Katz

Solomon Katz, President
PONCHO

THE CHILDREN'S ORTHOPEDIC HOSPITAL AND MEDICAL CENTER

Treuman Katz
Chief Executive Officer

T A M A L E   P I E

5 T butter	1 12-oz can whole tomatoes
1 c salad oil	1 12-oz can corn
2 medium onions	1 c milk
2 garlic cloves	1½ c ripe olives
3 T chili powder	1 T salt
1½ c corn meal	1 lb hamburger
3 eggs, beaten	

1. Melt butter in saute frying pan. Add the salad oil.

2. Cook onions and garlic cloves in butter and oil for 15 minutes.

3. Add tomatoes, corn, chili powder, corn meal, beaten eggs, olives, and salt, and cook for 15 minutes.

4. Brown hamburger in separate pan and add the hamburger to the above ingredients.

5. Place in buttered casserole dish and bake at 350° for 30 minutes.

From Chef Treuman Katz

The Seattle Times

FAIRVIEW AVENUE NORTH AND JOHN STREET
POST OFFICE BOX 70
SEATTLE, WASHINGTON 98111

Fastbreak Chicken

What does a sportswriter know about food?

We live in a world of hot dogs, peanuts and popcorn. Cuisine to
is chopped onions in the condiment bar. We exist on press box food.
Marathon runners carbo-load before a big race. We cholesterol load.
Our idea of a cocktail is Maalox on the rocks. A perfect dinner-date
is his and hers hoagies and a twi-night doubleheader.

Food? Who cares about food? We're too busy eating crow. We eat o
the run. A sitdown dinner for us has to be as fast as the Los Angeles
Laker fastbreak. Before a game, I like to dine on Fastbreak Chicken.

Starting lineup: 4 chicken breasts/ remove skin and fat; 1 egg,
beaten as fiercely as Marvin Hagler beat Thomas Hearns; 2 cups of
parmesan cheese; one package of Uncle Dan's Southern-style salad
dressing; dry paprika.

Game plan: Mix parmesan cheese and Uncle Dan's in medium-size
bowl. Dip chicken in egg and coat with parmesan cheese mix. Place in
a shallow pan and sprinkle with paprika. Bake at 425 degrees for 45
minutes-to-an-hour. Serve with baked potato and broccoli and eat
quickly. The game is about to start.

                              Steve Kelley

RED ROBIN
INTERNATIONAL

Dear Friends of Children's Orthopedic Hospital:

One of my favorite sports is skiing. Every year my wife Kathy and I go to Sun Valley where the snow is superb. A couple of years ago we ventured into one of our favorite restaurant haunts over there and on the menu was "Fireworks Shrimp". Since I love spicy foods, I ordered it and it quickly became one of my favorites. I was able to obtain the recipe from them and now I would like to share it with you. Enjoy!

FIREWORKS SHRIMP

(March 1982)

1 lb. medium shrimp - shelled & deveined
1/3-½ tsp. fresh garlic - finely minced
3 tbsp. tomato sauce or puree
1 tbsp. oyster sauce
1 tsp. red wine vinegar
½ tsp. sugar
¼ lb. snow peas - trimmed

3 garlic cloves - finely minced
½ tbsp. chili paste with garlic
2 tbsp. dry sherry
1 tbsp. light soy sauce
1 tsp. sesame oil
2 tbsp. peanut oil

4 bok choy - (chinese cabbage) stalks, cut diagonally into 1½-inch pieces.
3 green onions - cut diagonally into 3-inch pieces
2 tbsp. cornstarch mixed with 3 tbsp. of cold water

Cut shrimp in half lengthwise and set aside. Combine minced garlic, ginger and chili paste in a small bowl and set aside. Blend tomato sauce, sherry, oyster sauce, soy sauce, vinegar, sesame oil and sugar in another bowl.

Heat wok until very hot over high heat. Add one tablespoon of peanut oil and coat sides of wok. When oil just begins to smoke, add shrimp and stir fry only until translucent. Tip shrimp out onto a plate and cover with wok top.

Immediately return the wok to high heat. Add remaining peanut oil and roll coat sides of wok. Add garlic mixture, snow peas, bok choy and green onions and stir fry until snow peas turn bright green.

Pour sauce around sides of wok. Return shrimp to wok, stir in as much of the cornstarch solution as needed to thicken the mixture. Taste and adjust seasoning. Serve immediately.

Sincerely,

Gerald R. Kingen

Corporate Headquarters: 3123 Eastlake Avenue East, Seattle, WA 98102 • (206) 322-2246

| RED ROBIN BURGER & SPIRITS EMPORIUMS | BOONDOCK'S SUNDECKER'S & GREENTHUMB'S | LAKE UNION CAFE | LION O'REILLY'S & B.J. MONKEYSHINE'S | SALTY'S OF PORTLAND | SALTY'S AT REDONDO |

RESTAURANTS UNLIMITED

CHICKEN BREASTS WITH PASTA AND OLIVES

2 servings

        1/4 cup olive oil
    1 medium onion, chopped
    1 to 2 garlic cloves,
            minced
        1 teaspoon salt
      1 teaspoon turmeric
       1 teaspoon cumin
    1/4 teaspoon cayenne
            pepper
    2 whole chicken breasts
      1 8¼-ounce can whole
      tomatoes, cut into
    quarters, liquid reserved
       3 mushrooms, sliced
      1 2.2-ounce can sliced
       black olives, drained
    1/4 to 1/2 cup dry white wine
    Freshly cooked spaghettini

Heat oil in medium skillet over medium-
high heat. Add onion and garlic and saute
until translucent, about 5 minutes. Stir
in salt, turmeric, cumin and cayenne. Add
chicken and cook until light golden, about
3 minutes per side. Stir in tomatoes with
liquid, mushrooms and olives. Add 1/4 cup
wine. Reduce heat to low, cover partially
and cook until juices run clear when chicken
is pierced with tip of sharp knife, 35 to
40 minutes, adding more wine as necessary
to keep moist. Serve immediately over pasta.

                Richard B. Komen, Chairman

1818 N. NORTHLAKE WAY / SEATTLE, WASHINGTON 98103 / (206) 634-0550

CIOPPINO

Cook in a large pot for 10 minutes:

    1/2 cup oil
    1 clove garlic
    1 cup chopped onion or leek
    1 cup of chopped green onions
    1/2 cup chopped green (or red) pepper

Drain off extra oil. Add and simmer for at least 45 minutes:

    2 or 3 bay leaves
    1 8 oz. can tomato paste
    1 large can tomatoes
    2 cups red wine
    1/2 cup sherry
    1 teaspoon salt
    1/4 teaspoon oregano
    pinch of basil
    pepper
    1/4 cup parsley (optional)

Add combination of fresh fish of your choice and cook no more than
3 to 4 minutes or until clams open:

    2 dozen fresh clams in shell (scrubbed)
    1 Dungeness crab in shell (broken and partly cracked)
    1 lb. cooked shrimp
    1 lb. fresh scallops
    1/2 lb. salmon filet, cubed
    1/2 lb. white fish (cod, snapper, etc.), cubed
    mussels

Be sure not to overcook fish. Serve in large bowls. Serves 4-6.
Good with sourdough bread.

(This recipe was shared by Shelby Gilje several years ago at a New
Year's Eve potluck at a cabin near Anacortes. It has been a
favorite ever since.)

Polly Lane
Polly Lane

Good Company

A Production of KING Television   333 Dexter Avenue North   P.O. Box 24525   Seattle, Washington 98124   206/343-3781

WORLD'S MOST SCRUMPTIOUS HOT BUTTERED RUM MIX

CONCOCTED BY CLIFF AND LANA RAE LENZ*

1 PT. VANILLA ICE CREAM (FRATELLI'S IS PARTICULARLY GOOD)
1 C. BUTTER
2 C. BROWN SUGAR
2 t. CINNAMON
2 t. NUTMEG
1 C. POWDERED SUGAR

IN A FOOD PROCESSOR USING A STEEL BLADE, BLEND ICE CREAM AND BUTTE
UNTIL SMOOTH. ADD BROWN SUGAR, CINNAMON, NUTMEG AND POWDERED SUGA
AND THEN BLEND WELL.
ADD ONE MORE CUP OF POWDERED SUGAR AND BLEND. IF BATTER IS TOO ST
FOR PROCESSOR, BLEND BY HAND.
KEEP REFRIGERATED OR MAY BE FROZEN IF MADE IN ADVANCE OF USE.

* THE CONTRIBUTION OF MY WIFE IN THE CREATION OF THIS RECIPE CANNO
  AND MUST NOT BE UNDERESTIMATED.

A Division of King Broadcasting Company

Irving M. Levine 300 - 120th Avenue Northeast, Bellevue, Washington 98005

HERRING ANTIPASTO

1 Jar Lasco Wine Herring Snacks - 6 oz.

1 Medium to large onion, chopped fine

1 Medium green pepper, chopped fine

1 7 oz. can pitted black olives, chopped fine

*1 Jar "Homemade Chili Sauce"

In a large bowl, cut herring snacks in small bite
size pieces. Add chopped onion, green pepper and
olives.

Stir in entire jar of chili sauce and refrigerate.

Serve in bowl with rye bread sliced thin and quartered.

*"Home Made Chili Sauce"is the brand name and can be
  found on the grocery shelves in a small round jar.

(This recipe does not work well in the Cuisinart, but
 is worth chopping by hand. It's a crowd pleaser and
 keeps for two weeks refrigerated.)

                            Mrs. Irving J. Levine

CHICKEN PAPRIKA

2 teaspoons sesame seed or safflower oil

1 onion, chopped, small

1 bell pepper (optional), small, diced

1/2 teaspoon whole dried marjoram

1½ tablespoons Hungarian-style paprika

4 chicken breasts

3/4 cup chicken broth

3 oz. Neufchatel low-fat cream cheese

1 teaspoon arrowroot

Garnish - parsley or scallions

Preheat oven to 350°. In heavy skillet, heat oil and gently
saute onion and bell pepper. Sprinkle with marjoram and
1 tablespoon paprika. Stir. No sticking allowed. Sprinkle
remaining paprika over chicken breasts and place breasts over
onions. Cover and bake 35 to 40 minutes.

Remove from oven. Add chicken broth and simmer 2 to 3 minutes.
Remove breasts. Blend broth, onions, cheese and arrowroot in
blender. Replace chicken breasts in skillet; pour sauce over
chicken and cook about 5 minutes to reduce. Season and garnish.

The wonderful thing about this
recipe is that the sauce looks
and tastes like a rich cream sauce
but is actually low in calories.

Carol Lewis
Deputy Mayor

An equal employment opportunity - affirmative action employer.
1200 Municipal Building, Seattle, Washington 98104, (206) 625-4000

90

Seattle King County Council
8511 15th Ave NE. Seattle. WA 98115
Phone (206) 524-8550

Board of Directors
Officers
President
Gary R. Neumann
Past President
William R. Bannecker
First Vice President
Robert W. Evans
Second Vice President
Frances Shintaku
Third Vice President
Nancy McReynolds
Secretary
Judy Weisfield
Treasurer
Dean Saffle

Members
Margaret Bernard
Earline Bowen
Doris A. Cairns
Jean M. Cerar
JoAnn M. Clark
Joyce Clark
Sandy Ekins
Susan Finneran
Judy Fischer
Kristen Girod
Charly Parker-Glock
Catherine ("Mike") Hayes
Charles A. Heinrich
Susan Hogan
Marjorie Kettells
Gary Locke
Jan Loughney
Carman Milnor
Ronald D. Olstad
Shirley Probasco
Ann Putnam
John L. Robins
Pinckney M. Rohrback
Kristin Ross
Lael Ross
M. Lynn Ryder
Orv Simpson
Cynthia P. Sonstelie
Michele M. Thomas
Delna Vermillion
Lisa Washington
Sue Wescott

Honorary Board Members
Majorie McCrory
George Parsons

Board Consultants
Jane McKelvy
Bradley C. Diggs

Executive Director
Patricia F. Lewis, CFRE

Assistant Executive Director
Joan Bergesen

A very special friend, Sophia Levendoski, taught me how to make these marvelous cookies, now a family tradition for any celebration. The recipe was brought to this country from Poland by her mother in the late 1800's. The cookies are wonderful if evaporated milk is substituted for the cream and shortening for the butter; they are extraordinary if made as presented. We often use local berry preserves for the filling.

Croatian Yeast Cookies

In medium bowl, mix:
    2 c. sifted flour
    3/4 t. baking powder
Cut in, to form crumbs, like pie crust:
    1/2 c. butter
    2 T shortening

In small bowl, beat:
    2 egg yolks
Add to:
    1/2 c. sour cream (or sweet)
Soften & blend together:
    1 yeast cake
    2 T cream (or water)

Add the liquid ingredients to the flour mixture; makes a soft dough. Chill 2 – 3 hours. Roll out to approx. 1/8" thick on sugared flour board. Cut into 2" squares. Spread 1/2 t. filling across each square diagonally. Pull other 2 corners over the filling & pinch together. Bake 10 min., 450 degree oven.

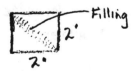 

Fillings

1 c. strawberry or blackberry preserves, or
1 c. orange marmalade mixed with 1/4 c. ground walnuts, or
Blend together:
    1/2 c. finely ground nuts
    1/8 t. cinnamon
    1 stiffly beaten egg white
    5 T sugar
    1 T hot milk

Pat Lewis

A United Way Agency

75 YEARS

Rainier Brewing Company

P.O. BOX 24828, SEATTLE, WASHINGTON 98124

John H. Lindsay
Executive Vice President

What a wonderful idea!

As long time supporters of the activities and services of Children's Orthopedic Hospital and Medical Center, we salute your fundraising cookbook project. And we gladly submit our Rainier Beer Cheese Recipe for inclusion in the book.

We used to serve the cheese in our hospitality room to all the visitors who stopped by for a tour. Even though we haven't provided it for many years, people still write to us requesting the recipe.

BEER CHEESE

1 lb. medium sharp cheese
   (approx. 4 cups ground)
1 tsp. garlic salt
2 tsp. minced onion

1 tsp. dry mustard
   dash tabasco
1 tsp. Worcestershire
1 T butter

8 oz. Rainier Beer

Grind or grate cheese. Place all ingredients except beer in mixer bowl. Gradually add beer and beat until smooth and fluffy. Store in covered container in refrigerator. Serve at room temperature with crackers or dark bread.

Yield: 1 quart

GARY LOCKWOOD'S WORLD FAMOUS

BARBECUED CHICKEN

Two chickens (cut up)
Worchestershire sauce
Butter (cube)
Johnny's Seasoning Salt
Pepper
Large bottle of brand name barbecue sauce

Pour entire bottle of barbecue sauce into a medium/large sauce pan.
Add two cubes of butter. (NOT MARGARINE)
One teaspoon of Johnny's Salt.
One teaspoon of pepper.
Four tablespoons of worchestershire sauce.
Heat on medium temperature until cubes of butter are melted. (Be sure to stir occasionally)

Place chickens on grill over hot coals.
With brush, baste every piece of chicken generously.
Immediately flip chicken with basted side down. (The sauce will drip down onto the coals, so have a squirter or squirt gun ready to douse the flames. Otherwise the flames will BURN the chicken skin)
Let chicken cook for five minutes.
Baste the top and flip again.
Let chicken cook for five minutes.
Repeat this process for 45 minutes to an hour or whenever chicken is done.

Obviously you will have leftovers which you can refrigerate. They are delicious the next day.

Our headquarters was located in the International District for two years. We learned a lot about Chinese cuisine and this is one of my favorites.

HOT & SPICY CHICKEN

1 chicken breast
2 T chili paste*
1½ T dry sherry
2 T soy sauce
1 T peanut oil
1½ t sesame oil
2 green onions (cut into 2" pieces)
1 green pepper (chopped)
1 stalk of broccoli (cut into bite size pieces)
1 c fresh mushrooms (sliced)
½ c raw peanuts or almonds
¼ c chicken broth or 1 bouillion cube dissolved in
    water

Skin and bone chicken and cut into strips. Combine chili paste, sherry and soy sauce and marinate chicken for 30 minutes or more. Heat oil in wok or skillet. Drain chicken and stir fry in oil quickly until white and remove. Stir fry onions, peppers and broccoli for one minute. Add mushrooms, peanuts and chicken and stir fry for another minute. Add marinade and stock and stir to coat. Serve with rice.

*chili paste can be purchased at any Oriental
    market

Sincerely Yours,

Karen Marchioro
Democratic State Chair

SEATTLE SUPERSONICS

P.O. Box 900911
Seattle, WA 98109-9711

<u>BROCCOLI & CHICKEN CASSEROLE</u>

2 pkgs. broccoli spears
Pepperidge Farm Stuffing Mix- 2/3 cup
2 whole chicken breasts, cooked, boned & skinned.
1 can cream of mushroom soup
1 cup mayo
1 T. milk

Defrost broccoli spears and place in a 9x13 baking dish.
Sprinkle P. stuffing over the broccoli.

Arrange cooked chicken breasts over the broccoli and stuffing.

Mix mushroom soup, mayo and milk and pour over all.

Cover all with cheddar cheese. Bake at 350 25 minutes.

Jim and Linda Marsh

JOHN D. MARSHALL
COLUMNIST
628-8170

MARSHALL WILTED LETTUCE

1	Head of lettuce
6	Slices of bacon, cut in small pieces
3	Tablespoons of bacon fat
1/4	Cup of vinegar
1	Teaspoon of sugar
	Salt and pepper

Cut up lettuce in a bowl. Fry bacon in
fry pan until crisp, then remove. Leave
3 tablespoons of bacon fat in pan and heat.
Add vinegar to pan, sugar, plus salt and pepper
to taste; then heat. Pour over lettuce.
Toss with the bacon and serve at once.

This hot lettuce dish is a great dinner
alternative in the fall and winter when local
greens disappear from the market and when the
last thing one wants is a cold salad.

The beauty of this dish is that it's
simple, quick, indestructible and darn tasty.
Plus Marshall Wilted Lettuce can easily be
updated for today's Yuppie tastes. Use
spinach instead of lettuce. Try using
different wine or herb vinegars. Or experiment
by adding some shallots, garlic, mushrooms
or slivered almonds to the bacon fat and fry
lightly before tossing.

Marshall Wilted Lettuce goes back two
generations in our family to when the Marshalls
were living in Texas in the 1920s. I remember
my mother making this dish from a recipe
handwritten by my father's mother on a fading
piece of notepaper. My own copy of the recipe
was included in one of the last letters my
mother sent me before her death. So it has
both history and special meaning for me.

FROM THE KITCHEN OF ERNEST A. MARTINEZ

Tortellini Salad
(Serves 4-6)

1 pound frozen tortellini
1 tablespoon olive oil
1 head broccoli, cut into small flowerettes and blanched
2 cups cherry tomatoes, halved
1 cup mushrooms, thinly sliced
3/4 cup Dijon Vinaigrette*
Salt
Pepper

Bring 4-6 quarts of water to boil. Drop tortellini and stir with spoon to prevent from sticking. Cook until al dente, 3-4 minutes, stirring occasionally. Drain, then run under cold water to stop further cooking. Drain again and toss with olive oil. Mix tortellini with remaining ingredients.

*Dijon Vinaigrette
(Makes 3/4 cup)

2 tablespoons Dijon mustard
1/4 cup bottled oil and vinegar dressing.

Whisk mustard into dressing then pour over salad.

Ernest

SEATTLE CENTRAL
COMMUNITY COLLEGE
1701 BROADWAY • SEATTLE, WASHINGTON 98122

Gretchen's of course

ZITI WITH SAUSAGE SALAD

1/3 cup red wine vinegar
1/2 teaspoon salt
1/4 teaspoon freshly ground pepper
1/4 teaspoon dried rosemary, crumbled, or 1/2 teaspoon fresh rosemary
1/4 teaspoon dried oregano, crumbled, or 1/2 teaspoon fresh oregano, chopped
1/4 teaspoon dried basil, crumbled, or 1/2 teaspoon fresh basil, chopped
1 1/3 cups olive or vegetable oil or combination
1/4 cup freshly grated parmesan cheese
12 ounces ziti (pasta)
2 pounds cooked smoked sausage, thinly sliced (use Bavarian Meat Store Farmers
    Sausage)
1 pound zucchini, thinly sliced
4 medium tomatoes, cut into wedges
1 medium green bell pepper, coarsely chopped
1 cup minced fresh parsley
1 jar (3 ounces) pimiento, chopped
Freshly grated parmesan cheese

Combine vinegar, salt, pepper and herbs in small bowl. Whisk in oil in slow
steady stream until well blended. Mix in 1/4 cup parmesan cheese. Set aside.
Cook ziti in 4 to 6 quarts boiling salted water until just firm, but tender
to the bite, about 7 minutes. Drain and rinse under cold water until cool.
Drain again. Combine ziti and remaining ingredients except parmesan in large
bowl. Add half of dressing and toss. Add as much of the remaining dressing
as necessary to coat salad thoroughly. Sprinkle with additional grated
parmesan if desired.

An original from Gretchen's from the Pike Place Market days. A great salad
dressing with or without the rest of the ingredients. Such a popular salad
that I named my dog "Ziti" after it. She's a great Lab who loves pasta and
all the other ingredients except the veggies.

909 UNIVERSITY   SEATTLE WA 98101   TEL   623-8194
ALSO - 1111 THIRD AVE   94 STEWART   1513 SIXTH AVE   SEATTLE
ONE BELLEVUE CENTER - 411 108th N.E.   BELLEVUE

MIKE McCORMACK
PRESIDENT/GENERAL MANAGER

The McCormack family spent many years in Maryland and the Eastern shore area. This recipe comes from Annapolis and was always a favorite. It's easy and delicious.

BAKED SHRIMP AND RICE

1/3 cup chopped onion
2 tablespoons butter
1 or 2 cloves of garlic
2 pounds cooked shrimp
1 cup raw rice
3 cups stewed tomatoes
2 cups chicken stock
1 bay leaf
3 tablespoons chopped parsley
1/4 teaspoon cloves
1/2 teaspoon marjoram
1 teaspoon chili powder
2 teaspoon salt
1/8 teaspoon pepper
dash of cayenne

Brown onion in butter with garlic which has been put through press. Mix with shrimp and add all other ingredients in a large baking dish. Cover tightly and bake for 1½ hours in 350° oven.

Seattle Seahawks

5305 LAKE WASHINGTON BLVD • KIRKLAND, WA. 98033 • (206) 827-9777

THE WORLD B NUB 27 STEP
SPECIAL-RUBBER-NUBBER-AFTER-OR-BEFORE-EVERY-TV-BOWL-WORLD SERIES-
ANY-KIND-OF-VICE-(MIAMI)-OR-NATIONAL-CHAMPIONSHIP-SUNDAY-ONLY-OMELETTE

by
C. Clifford McCrath

1. Arise when neighborhood dogs start barking
2. Let your own dog out
3. Make coffee
4. Drink coffee
5. Tussel hair or toupee into place
6. Find the newspaper
7. Turn on stove
8. Find from 3 to 47 eggs
9. Place on counter next to stove
10. Warmup by catching eggs rolling off counter
11. Place ham, sausage, bacon, pepperoni, green pepper, 13 cheeses, saltine crackers, milk, mushrooms, sour cream, chives, salt, pepper (Krazy Jane or Sally, Mary, etc.) alongside cutting board
12. Cook sausage and bacon
13. Shred cheeses, chop up all other ingredients except milk and sour cream
14. Find appropriate non-stick, frying pan (regular if 3 egg omelette, basketball court size pan if 47 egg omelette)
15. Pour anywhere from a thimbleful to 35 quarts of corn oil (fat free) into pan
16. Heat until smoke alarm goes off
17. Mix eggs with wooden spoon (if 3 egg omelette) or cement mixer (if 47 egg omelette)
18. Add milk (one or 85 squirts)
19. Pour into pan and slush around until things look like they're happening
20. Begin sprinkling in all other ingredients (except sour cream) in any order that turns you on!
21. Grab handle and begin fencing (epee) movements similar to when you make popcorn in a frying pan
22. Once everything looks like it's finally getting together try the original pizza movement (if 3 egg omelette) by tossing entire mess into air (make sure pan has been removed from stove area otherwise fan vent costs $82.00 to get all ingredients cleaned out)
23. Try to catch omelette on reverse side (for gymnasts you may use spotter to guide airborn omelette)
24. Slide golden brown omelette onto plate (if 3 egg omelette) onto fork lift (if 47 egg omelette)
25. Serve with sour cream, toast, more coffee and melon wedges
26. Find a place to lie down
27. Let the dog in!

Athletic Department
Seattle Pacific University
Seattle, WA 98119
(206) 281-2085

100

SEATTLE SUPERSONICS

P.O. Box 900911
Seattle, WA 98109-9711

FRIED RICE WITH HAM

1 T. butter
½ cup fresh mushrooms
2 T. cooking oil
1½ cup long grain rice, cooked
2 green onion, thinly sliced length-wise
½ cup fresh bean sprouts
½ cup chopped onions
2 T. chopped green peppers
1 T. soy sauce
½ t. salt
dash pepper
1 T. light scotch whiskey (optional)
2 beaten eggs
½ cup fully cooked diced ham

Pre-heat large skillet. Melt butter and saute mushrooms until tender. Remove from pan.

Over high heat, add oil and stir fry rice for 2 minutes. Add green onions, mushrooms, ham, sprouts, onion and green pepper. Stir fry for 2 minutes.

Add soy, scotch, salt and pepper. Reduce to medium heat.

Move rice into a ring along the side of the skillet. Pour beaten eggs in the center and cook until set. When egg is completely cooked, mix all together with rice mixture.

Serve immediately!

Xavier and Sylvia McDaniel

Hugh McMenemy
4013 171 Ave. S.E.
Bellevue, Wash. 98008

My favorite <u>Irish Stew</u> recipe is as follows:

6 medium-sized peeled potatoes, cut crosswise into 1/4 inch slices
4 large onions, peeled and cut into 1/4 inch slices
3 pounds lean boneless lamb neck or shoulder, trimmed of all fat
  and cut into 1 inch cubes
1 teaspoon salt
Freshly ground black pepper
1/4 teaspoon thyme
Cold water

Spread half the potatoes on the bottom of a heavy 4 to 5 quart
casserole or Dutch oven, and cover them with half the onion slices
and then all the lamb. Sprinkle with 1/2 teaspoon of the salt,
a few grindings of pepper and the thyme. Arrange the rest of the
onions over the meat and spread the remaining potatoes on top.
Sprinkle with 1/2 teaspoon of salt and a few grindings of pepper,
then pour in enough cold water just to cover the potatoes.

Bring the stew to a boil over high heat, reduce the heat to its
lowest possible point, and cover the casserole tightly. Simmer
for 1½ hours. Check from time to time and add boiling water, a
tablespoon or two at a time, if the liquid seems to be cooking
away.

Serve the stew directly from the casserole or Dutch oven, ladling
it into deep heated individual serving bowls. Serves 4 to 6.

If you want a traditional Irish meal, serve the stew with
pickled red cabbage.

BRISKET OF BEEF

Preheat oven to 325 degrees.

4 to 5 pounds

4 cloves garlic - put through press
salt, pepper
Lowry's seasoning
paprika

Mix all of the above and spread on meat.

In bottom of roaster place 6 cut onions, salt, pepper and paprika. Place brisket on flat rack. Add 1 cup water, cover, baste. Cook 3 to 4 hours. You may need to add more water. Test for doneness. When done, take out meat. Put gravy through Foley Food Mill and refrigerate overnight.

Next day skim fat off gravy. Slice brisket. Place sliced brisket in flat pan. Pour heated gravy over all. May add 1 can mushrooms. Cover and heat in oven.

As a side dish serve noodles with the gravy or rice that has been warmed with the gravy.

Brisket may be done ahead of time and frozen. Freeze gravy separately. Defrost and heat together.

Fern Meltzer • 6210 s.e. twenty-second, mercer island, wa. 98040 •

Fern Meltzer was the founder and first president of the Seattle Chapter of City of Hope National Medical and Research Center. She has served as president of Brandeis University National Women's Committee and as a panel member for United Way. She and her daughter, Bobbie Stern, received special recognition last year for their fundraising efforts on behalf of City of Hope.

JOHN R. MILLER
1ST DISTRICT, WASHINGTON

COMMITTEES:
GOVERNMENT OPERATIONS
MERCHANT MARINE AND
FISHERIES

1723 LONGWORTH BUIL
WASHINGTON, DC 205
(202) 225-6311

DISTRICT OFFICE:
2888 FEDERAL BUILDIN
915 SECOND AVENUE
SEATTLE, WA 98174
(206) 442-4220

Congress of the United States
House of Representatives
Washington, DC 20515

NORWEGIAN BLØTKAKE (whipping cream cake)

Ingredients for the sponge cake base:

- 6 whole eggs
- 1 cup of sugar
- 2 t. baking powder
- 7 T. flour
- 5 T. potatoe flour
- 3 T. cold water

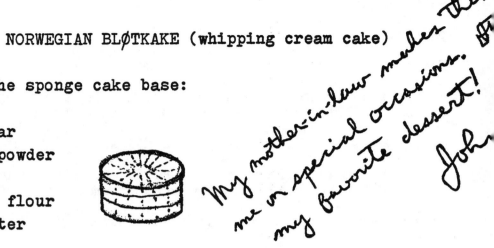

My mother-in-law makes this for me on special occasions. It's my favorite dessert! John

Divide the eggs and beat the egg whites til stiff. In another bowl put the egg yolks, sugar and water. Beat til the sugar is dissolved.

Sift flour, potatoe flour and baking powder. Add to the egg yolk mixture. Stir in the egg whites.

Bake on the middle rack in an ungreased 11" round spring pan. Put it in a cold oven and set temperature to 325 degrees. After 15 minutes raise the temperature to 350 degrees for 45 minutes.

When done, lift carefully from the oven. Use a sharp knife to separat cake from sides and spring away. After 15 minutes slide knife under cake and flip to a cooling rack. When cold, cut into 3 layers.

Beat 1 quart and 1 cup of whipping cream. Spread 2 T. strawberry jelly evenly on the bottom layer. Spread 1/3 of the whipping cream over the jelly. Spread 2 T. strawberry jelly on the middle layer <u>before</u> placing it on the completed bottom layer. Spread 1/3 of the whipping cream over middle layer. Take the last layer and place on top. With a sharp knife, make a 2" circle in the center of the cake. Then cut 14 slices of cake.

When all is cut, spread the remaining whipping cream over the top and sides of the cake. Cover with a cake cover and refrigerate 24 hours before serving. With a cake server the pieces will pull away beautifully.

When the editors of this cookbook invited me to contribute "one of my favorite recipes," I was more than happy to do so for the opportunity it provided to accomplish two worthwhile things.

The first worthwhile thing was to dispel the dangerous notion that I actually can cook.

And the second worthwhile thing was to reveal, to people generous enough to support Children's Orthopedic Hospital, one of the great culinary secrets of our time -- namely, how my wife makes her caramel bars.

It may seem incongruous for a distinguished hospital to be associated with something as devastating to the cause of a sensible diet as Mrs. Mooney's caramel bars. But after you've tried a plateful, I don't believe you'll hold it against Children's Orthopedic.

The ingredients:

> 2/3 cup evaporated milk, divided.
> 1 (14 oz.) bag vanilla caramels
> (approximately 44 caramels).
> 1 German Chocolate cake mix.
> 1 cup walnuts, chopped.
> 2/3 cup butter or margarine, melted.
> 6 oz. (1 cup) semi-sweet chocolate chips.

Directions: In top of double boiler or a heavy saucepan, melt caramels in 1/3 cup evaporated milk; set aside. Melt butter or margarine and mix with the dry cake mix, the walnuts and the remaining 1/3 cup evaporated milk. Press half of the cake mixture in the bottom of a greased 9-1/2 by 13 inch pan. Bake for six minutes at 350 degrees. Remove from oven, sprinkle the top with chocolate chips. Spoon melted caramel mixture over the chips. Press remaining cake mixture into flattened patties, covering the surface as well as you can. Bake at 350 degrees for 16 to 18 minutes. Cut when cool.

Bon Appetit!

Joe Mooney

Joe Mooney

WORKING PERSON'S SPAGHETTI SAUCE

2 lbs.	extra lean ground beef
1 -	medium-sized yellow onion, diced
3 tbs.	Market Spice Italian seasoning
1 -	32 oz. can of whole tomatoes
2 -	8 oz. cans of tomato sauce
1 -	4 oz. can of tomato paste
1 -	6 oz. can of mushrooms
2 -	medium-sized carrots, peeled and generously sliced
1 cup	red wine
2 -	cloves of garlic, mashed
1 -	dried red chili pepper

Brown ground beef in a skillet, sprinkle with Italian spice. Transfer to a large cooking pot. Brown onions in the same skillet, using ground beef drippings. Add onions with remaining ingredients to ground beef.

Cover pot and simmer for about three hours or until carrots are tender. Serve with pasta of your choice and fresh, grated parmesan.

Sauce is even better the second day. Can be made in a crockpot.

Submitted by Wendy Morgan, Executive Director, Bellevue Community College Foundation

A NONPROFIT ORGANIZATION PROMOTING EXCELLENCE IN EDUCATION
3000 Landerholm Circle S. E., P. O. Box 92700, Bellevue, WA 98009-2037   (206) 641-2282

106

UWAJIMAYA

6th Avenue South & South King Street / Seattle, Washington 98104 / (206) 624-6248
P.O. Box 3003 / Seattle, Washington 98114

Tomio Moriguchi, President

FRIED RICE

1 Tbsp. vegetable oil
2 eggs, beaten

3 strips bacon cut into ½ inch pieces
1 Chinese sausage, chopped
1 small onion, chopped
1 cup bean sprouts
3 cups cooked long grain rice
2 Tbsp. soy sauce
2 tsp. sesame seed oil
¼ cup chopped green onions

1. Heat the wok and add 1 tablespoon of oil. Stir fry eggs until done and remove. Set aside.

2. Add the bacon to the wok and cook until most of the fat is rendered. Remove the fat from the wok.

3. Add the Chinese sausage and stir fry for ½ minute. Add the chopped onions and bean sprouts. Cook for ½ minute.

4. Add the rice and fry until hot, turning down the temperature if necessary.

5. Add the soy sauce and sesame seed oil. Continue to fry until the rice is of even color.

6. Add the eggs and green onions; mix all ingredients together breaking the eggs into small pieces. Serve hot.

This recipe is delicious as a complete meal or as a side dish.

Groceries and gifts from the east and west.

JACK MORTON.....AN OLDER RADIO PERSON.....EXCEPT FOR JIM FRENCH!

DETENTE SANDWICH

<u>Russian</u> Rye Bread (key ingredient)

<u>American</u> Cheese

Cold, Crisp Cucumbers (sliced to desired thickness)

Walla Walla Sweet Onions (you <u>must</u> use Walla Walla's)

Layer of Mayonnaise

Salt and Pepper to Taste

Jack Morton

Donald R. Olson
Administrator

VIRGINIA MASON HOSPITAL

Bouillabaisse

1 carrot, diced

2 onions chopped

2 leeks (white part only) or 4 green onions

1 clove garlic, crushed

1/2 cup olive oil

3 pounds white fish, cut in 3" pieces

2 large tomatoes (or 1 cup canned tomatoes)

Salt and pepper to taste

1 Bay leaf

2 cups fish stock, clam juice or water

1 cup cooked shrimp, crab or lobster

2 dozen scrubbed oysters or clams

1 can (4 oz.) pimientos

Juice of 1 lemon

1 cup dry white wine or sherry

Cook first four ingredients in oil in large kettle until golden brown. Add fish, tomatoes, salt and pepper, bay leaf and stock. Bring to boil, cover and simmer 20 minutes. Add shellfish and simmer 5 minutes or until shells open. Add remaining ingredients. Heat well.

Don't forget--the origin of Bouillabaisse was the Mediterranean and the creativity of the cook making "something out of nothing"--the real fun is being your own cook with the suggested start above. You will miss the real formula if you don't experiment and make this your own recipe--have fun!

925 Seneca Street
P.O. Box 1930
Seattle, Washington 98111
(206) 624-1144

The Intermediate Eate

*John
Owen*

Box 1281

Bellevue, WA 98009

McCAUSLAND

Fish Stew Seattle

1 small onion, finely chopped
1 can (No. 2 1/2) tomatoes
2 tablespoons chili sauce
1/4 tea. Italian herbs
1/4 tea. paprika
1 minced clove garlic
1/2 tea. salt
3 tablespoons olive oil
4 chopped stalks celery
1/4 tea. dry mustard
1 cup dry, white wine
2 carrots, chopped
1 tablespoon brown sugar
1/4 tea. celery salt
16 prawns
2 lbs. clams in shell
1 lb. red snapper
pint of clam nectar or chicken bouillon

Saute the onions and garlic in the hot oil in a large soup pot. When soft add all the other ingredients EXCEPT the fish, prawns and clams.

Let the stock simmer for at least an hour. Shell prawns and remove black vein from the back. Brush the clams under cold water to insure you don't have any booby traps (which act like clams, but actually consist of one tablespoon black sand.)

When your hour is up, add the red snapper in chunks and toss in the prawns. Let the stew simmer another 15 minutes, then plunk in the clams. Cover pot, simmer another 10 to 15 minutes until all the clams have opened, then serve.

Salsa di Buggiano

6 hot Italian sausage links
1 large onion, chopped or minced
1 carrot, grated
1 Bell pepper
1 stalk celery
1 large (28-oz.) can tomatoes
2 large (28-oz.) cans tomato sauce
1 6-oz. can tomato paste
2 cups Hearty Burgundy
1 cup water
3 cloves garlic (or more) sliced thin

Brown sausage in a little olive oil in a large stainless
steel pot. Remove, and add onion and carrot. Saute until soft.
Put celery, green pepper and tomatoes through processor. Add
to pot with remaining ingredients. Return sausage to sauce and
add sliced raw garlic. Simmer for several hours. Serve over
pasta or polenta (corn meal mush.)

Augusto Paglialunga
Associate Professor
School of Music
International Opera Singer

Restaurant Français

Gerard Parrat

Gerard's Relais de Lyon

17121 Bothel Way N.E.
P.O. Box 733
Bothel, Washington 98011
(206) 485-7600

Iles Flottantes

1 quart of milk
2 cups of granulated sugar
12 egg yolks
1 T vanilla
1 t corn starch

Mix sugar and egg yolks. Add vanilla. Bring the milk to a boil. Pour into sugar and egg mixture. Return to heat and stir with spatula to almost boiling. Strain into cool container, and cool, stirring occasionally.

Now beat 8 egg whites to stiff peaks. Add ½ cup sugar. Form islands and poach in almost boiling water, 1 minute on each side.

Put sauce in serving dish. Add floating islands. Decorate with caramel.

Soupe de Poisson

1 quart of fish stock
2 medium carrots
2 stalks of celery
1 medium onion
1 pinch saffron
½ cup of white wine

1 clove of garlic
1 medium potato
2 t chervil or chives
2 T olive oil
salt and pepper to taste
croutons rubbed with garlic

Chop carrots, celery and onion in food processor. Saute vegetables in olive oil. Add saffron and continue to saute. Add white wine and cook for about 3 minutes. Add fish stock and boil until vegetables are tender. Boil potato in separate pan until cooked. Process with garlic clove to form a paste. Mix paste slowly into soup mixture, salt and pepper to taste, bring to boil and pour into soup tureen. Add chervil or chives and croutons on top. Serve right away.

Serves 4 people.

Fruit Soup

Serves 4 to 6

Combine in blender:

3 cups apple or pineapple juice
1 banana
1 chopped peeled apple
½ tsp. mint or dried mint
Juice from 1 lemon
1 chopped, peeled peach
Pieces of fresh cantaloupe
1 Tbs. honey (to taste)
1 cup yogurt
Dash of nutmeg

Thicken with more banana.
Thin with more juice.
Chill ½ hour or more.
Garnish with mint.

Robert Henry Pratt, Jr.

Seattle Seahawks

5305 LAKE WASHINGTON BLVD • KIRKLAND, WA. 98033 • (206) 827-9777

First Interstate Bank

First Interstate Bank
of Washington, N.A.
P.O. Box 160
Seattle, WA 98111

William S. Randall
President &
Chief Executive Officer

GRILLED HALIBUT WITH WHITE WINE AND CREAM
(any firm white fleshed fish is suitable)

4-5 oz. Halibut
White fish stock - Halibut bones and trim

1 part dry white wine
1 part cream
2 parts reduced fish stock - reduced by 1/2
Green, Red, Yellow pepper
Dijon mustard
Bread Crumbs
Lemon zest and juice
Parsley
Dill
White pepper

Grill or pan fry fillet in clarified butter or olive
oil on both sides.

Brush top of fillet with dijon mustard. Combine
melted butter, bread crumbs, finely minced zest of
lemon, finely chopped parsley and dill. Bake in
moderate oven for 10 to 15 minutes.

Sauce: Prepare sauce by reducing the white wine,
cream and fish stock by half - separately. Keep
warm and when fish is ready combine to form a sauce
with a thick consistency. Adjust seasoning with
salt and white pepper and undersauce the fillet of
halibut.

Garnish with blanched julienne of peppers in equal
parts.

This recipe is excellent with roast
wild duck or roast rack of lamb.

WILD RICE STUFFING

1-1/3 to 1-1/2 cups wild rice (8 oz.)
3/4 cup long grain white rice
1-1/2 sticks (12 Tbs.) unsalted butter
1/4 cup <u>each</u> finely chopped onions, carrots, celery
1/2 lb. mushrooms, sliced thin and sauteed in --
2 Tbs. butter
3 cups beef stock or bouillon
1-1/4 to 1-1/2 tsp. salt
1/2 tsp. thyme
1 bay leaf
2/3 cup dark raisins, soaked in 1/3 cup beef stock or bouillon
    for 20 minutes
2/3 cup walnuts, coarsely chopped and lightly sauteed in --
2 Tbs. unsalted butter
1 cup cooked breakfast sausage, drained and crumbled (i.e. Jimmy
    Dean original).

1. Add the wild rice to 3 qts. of boiling water and boil
uncovered for five minutes. Drain well.

2. While the rice is cooking, melt 1-1/2 sticks butter in a large
heavy casserole over moderate heat. Add the chopped celery,
carrots and onions and cook for 5-6 minutes until they are
tender. Add the sliced sauteed mushrooms to the vegetables. Add
the drained wild rice and the white rice. Toss to coat all
ingredients with the butter.

3. Add the beef stock, salt, thyme and bay leaf to the mixture.
Bring to a simmer on top of the stove and cover. Place in a
preheated 350 degree oven. Bake approximately 40 minutes and
remove from the oven. Add the raisins, walnuts and sausage and
toss well. Check seasonings. Return to the oven and cook 10
minutes more or until all the liquid has been absorbed.

Note: The rice and vegetables can be cooked in advance. When
ready to bake, add the bouillon and continue with recipe. The
rice will hold for up to an hour in a low oven.

Michael W. Rayden
President

KINGTV5 333 Dexter Avenue North
P.O. Box 24525
Seattle, Washington 98124
206/343-3000
A Division of King Broadcasting Company

<u>SAUTEED ABALONE</u>

One of my favorite off-air activities is scuba diving, particularly in the San Juan islands. The San Juans are home to that seafood delicacy known as the abalone. Smaller than their California cousins, our northwest variety lacks nothing in taste. My favorite preparation technique is to quickly saute them.

    1-2 Abalones per person
    1 cup flour
    4 eggs
    ½ cup beer or ale
    cracker crumbs

Tenderize the abalones with a tenderizing mallet after slicing them horizontally as thinly as possible. Be careful to tenderize, but not to tear the flesh. Placing the slices between sheets of waxed paper helps. Spread out the flour on a wooden carving board, and dust the abalone slices on both sides. Mix the eggs and beer, dip the abalone slices in the batter, then roll until sufficiently covered in the cracker crumbs. Drop them into a frying pan or wok filled with good cooking oil, and fry about 45 seconds to a minute-just until they turn golden brown. It's important not to overcook them, because that toughens the abalone. Enjoy them...they're scarce... but unbeatably delicious.

RUTHE RIDDER
KING COUNTY ASSESSOR

708 King County Administration Building
500 Fourth Avenue
Seattle, Washington 98104-2384

This was a prize-winning recipe when whole crabs were 39¢ a pound
- one crab provided just the right amount! Fortunately it also
works well with sole, snapper, salmon and tuna. Because it sits
overnight, the souffle is a good make-ahead company dish. One
year we served it to company, ate leftovers the second night, and
the third night found it at someone else's party - we _still_ enjoyed
the combination of flavor and texture.

Crab Souffle
(Yield 12 servings)

```
8    slices of bread
2    cups crab or shrimp
½    cup mayonnaise
1    onion, chopped
1    green pepper, chopped
1    cup celery, chopped
3    cups milk
4    eggs
1    can mushroom soup
     Grated cheese
     Paprika
```

1. Dice half of bread into baking dish. Mix crab or shrimp, mayonnaise,
onion, green pepper and celery. Spread over diced bread.

2. Trim crusts from remaining four slices and place trimmed slices
over crab mixture.

3. Mix eggs and milk together and pour over mixture. Place in
refrigerator overnight.

4. Bake at 325 degrees for 15 minutes. Remove from oven and spoon
soup over the top. Top with cheese and paprika.

5. Bake for an hour longer at 325 degrees. Serve immediately.

ROSELLINI'S FOUR-10
FOURTH & WALL ST.
SEATTLE, WA 98121
PHONE (206) 624-5464

ROSELLINI'S OTHER PLACE
319 UNION STREET
SEATTLE, WA 98101
PHONE (206) 623-7340

ROSELLINI'S OTHER PLACE

FETTUCCINI WITH TOMATO, BASIL & MUSHROOMS

SERVES 4

2 cups cream
2 tablespoons fresh chopped basil
3 cloves garlic, finely chopped
1 cup sliced mushrooms
1/4 teaspoon salt
1 medium tomato, peeled, seeded, diced
1/2 cup parmesan cheese, grated

1 pound fresh fettuccini
1 gallon water
1 tablespoon salt

In large, shallow sauce pan, combine cream, basil,
garlic, mushrooms and salt.
Reduce until thick.

Cook pasta in boiling salted water until barely tender.
Drain all water from pasta. Return pasta to same pan
and toss with thickened cream mixture and diced tomato
until pasta is well-coated with sauce.

Taste for seasoning.

Top with grated parmesan. Serve immediately.

ROBERT ROSELLINI

THIRD & WALL STREET / SEATTLE, WASH. 98121 / (206) 624-1761

ROSELLINI'S FOUR-10
FOURTH & WALL ST.
SEATTLE, WA 98121
PHONE (206) 624-5464

ROSELLINI'S OTHER PLACE
319 UNION STREET
SEATTLE, WA 98101
PHONE (206) 623-7340

VEAL SCALLOPINE - serving 4

Veal scallops - approximately 3 - 3½ oz. per person.
1 oz. oil
1½ oz. butter
½ cup all purpose flour
½ tsp salt
5 - 6 grinds fresh pepper

one lemon
white wine - 1 oz.
capers   - 1 tablespoon

Place veal between sheets of plastic. Pound <u>gently</u>.
Dust veal lightly with flour. Season with salt and pepper.
Heat oil over medium-high heat in heavy frying pan.
Brown veal quickly on each side. Transfer to heated
serving dish. Drain oil from pan. Deglaze pan with
wine (1 or 2 minutes). Add butter, capers, and lemon,
cut in half, juice squeezed over veal, dropping lemon
halves into pan. Cook until sauce thickens. Turn heat
to low, add veal, basting with sauce once or twice.
Discard lemon halves.
Transfer to serving dish.
Serve immediately.

**

The recipe for veal scallopine is one of our favorites,
for serving at the restaurant and also at home. It is
a simple, delicious preparation for veal - most enjoyable.

                                        VICTOR ROSELLINI

GERTRUDE'S CHEESE PIE

Ingredients:

    2/3 stick butter or oleo
    1-1/3 cups graham cracker crumbs
    3 tablespoons sugar
    4 large eggs, separated (or 5 medium or 6 small)
    1 cup sugar
    1 teaspoon vanilla
    3-8 ounce packages Philadelphia Cream Cheese

Melt butter or oleo and mix with graham cracker crumbs and 3 tablespoons sugar. Pat mixture in bottom of 10" springform pan.

Beat egg whites and set aside.

Combine egg yolks, 1 cup sugar, vanilla and Philadelphia Cream Cheese - beat until smooth. Gently fold in egg whites.

Pour mixture into graham cracker-lined springform pan and bake at 350° for 30-45 minutes.

Cool and freeze. Remove from freezer 45 minutes before serving.

Michael B. Rothenberg, M.D.

I am happy to share with you a favorite recipe used frequently in my home.

CHICKEN WITH JICAMA AND ORANGE

2 whole medium chicken breasts (about 1 1/2 lbs.) skinned, split lengthwise, and boned
6 tablespoons soy sauce
4 teaspoons cornstarch
1 teaspoon finely shredded orange peel
1 cup orange juice
1 6-ounce package frozen pea pods
2 tablespoons cooking oil
10 ounces jicama, peeled and cut into julienne strips (1 2/3 cups)
   Hot Cooked Rice

Cut chicken into 1-inch pieces; set aside. Combine soy sauce and cornstarch; stir in the orange peel and juice. Set aside. Run hot water over pea pods to thaw; drain. Heat oil in a wok or large skillet over high heat. Add jicama and pea pods; stir-fry 1 minute. Remove from wok. Add more oil, if necessary. Add half of the chicken to hot wok or skillet; stir-fry 2 minutes. Remove from wok. Stir-fry remaining chicken 2 minutes. Return all chicken to wok. Stir the soy-orange mixture; stir into chicken. Cook and stir till bubbly. Stir in jicama and pea pods. Cover, cook 1 minute more. Serve with rice. Serves 4.

Sincerely,

Barbara J Rothstein

Barbara J. Rothstein

Peanut Butter Chicken

4 chicken breasts
2 small bell peppers (1 red, 1 green)
3 medium size tomatoes
1/2 large white onion

1 t. salt
1 t. curry powder
1/4 c. oil
1/4 c. peanut butter
     (crunchy)
1/4 c. water
pepper to taste

Cut peppers into 1/4" strips
Peel and slice tomatoes
Slice onion thinly

In oil, brown chicken breasts in large frying pan. When brown, remove and stir into hot oil the salt and curry. Add onion, tomatoes and pepper and stir. Replace chicken and cover. Simmer on low heat for 20 minutes.

Remove chicken and keep warm. Mix peanut butter and water. Add mixture to vegetables while bringing to a boil. Reduce heat, replace chicken and cover for 10 minutes.

Serve with brown or white rice, spooning sauce over chicken and rice.

Serves 4.

An equal employment opportunity · affirmative action employer.
1200 Municipal Building, Seattle, Washington 98104, (206) 625-4000

122

CHICKEN PARMESAN WITH
NOODLES AND CHEESE

1 package (12 ounces) egg noodles
1 cup spaghetti sauce
¼ cup all-purpose flour
  Pinch pepper
1 egg, slightly beaten
1 tablespoon water
½ cup packaged seasoned bread crumbs
¼ cup grated Parmesan cheese
½ teaspoon leaf oregano, crumbled
4 boneless skinned chicken breast halves (1¼ pounds), lightly flattened
2 tablespoons olive oil
1 cup shredded mozzarella cheese (4 ounces)
1 tablespoon butter
¼ cup heavy cream
  Dash white pepper

1. Cook noodles following package directions.
2. Heat spaghetti sauce in small saucepan over low heat.
3. Combine flour and pepper on wax paper. Combine egg and water in shallow dish. Combine bread crumbs, 2 tablespoons of the Parmesan and oregano on second piece of wax paper.
4. Turn chicken in flour mixture to coat both sides evenly. Dip chicken in egg mixture, then crumbs, turning to coat all sides.
5. Heat oil in large skillet over high heat. Sauté chicken on one side for 3 minutes in hot oil or until lightly browned. Turn and sauté 2 minutes longer.
6. Lower heat to medium. Sprinkle mozzarella over chicken. Cover skillet and cook 2 minutes or until cheese is melted and chicken firm to the touch.
7. Meanwhile, drain noodles. Add butter and cream to pot used to cook noodles. Heat over medium heat until butter is melted and cream is bubbly. Add noodles, remaining Parmesan and white pepper; toss to combine.
8. Pour noodles onto serving platter; sprinkle with additional Parmesan; if you wish. Arrange chicken over noodles and spoon spaghetti sauce over chicken.

Makes 4 servings.

–Andy Russo

Andy Russo

faye sarkowsky

C A R M E L I T A S

1 Cup plus 3 tbsp. Unsifted Flour

1 Cup uncooked, quick oats

3/4 Cup Brown Sugar

1/2 Tsp. Baking Soda

3/4 Cup Melted Butter

1 Tsp. Salt

1 - 12 oz. Jar Caramel Topping

1 - 6 oz. Pkg. Chocolate Chips

1/2 Cup Chopped Nuts

Mix 1 cup flour and next 5 ingredients. Beat til well mixed. Evenly pat into ungreased 13" x 9" baking dish. Bake 10 minutes @ 350°.

Meanwhile, stir caramel topping and 3 tbsp. flour til mixed. Remove pan from oven. Sprinkle on chocolate chips and nuts. Drizzle on caramel mixture. Return pan to oven and continue baking another 20 - 25 minutes. Cool before cutting into squares.

Mary Quant

Freezes well.

HERMAN SARKOWSKY

3330 RAINIER BANK TOWER, SEATTLE, WASHINGTON 98101

Winter Barley Soup

2 1/2 Pounds Lamb Stew Meat
cut in 1 1/2-in chunks

2 tablespoons butter or
margarine

1/2 cup barley

2 medium onions, sliced

2 tablespoons chopped parsley

2 teaspoon salt

1/4 teaspoon pepper

1 bay leaf

1 1/2 cups chopped celery

1 1/2 cups carrots(Sliced)

1/2 Medium green pepper (Optional)

1/4 teaspoon thyme leaves

About 2 1/2 hours before serving:

In dutch oven over medium-high heat, brown lamb in butter or margarine;
add 6 cups hot water and next 6 ingredients. Simmer, covered, over medium-low
heat about 1 1/2 hours.

Stir in remaining sliced onion and the rest of the ingredients and cook
30 minutes or until meat is tender. Remove bay leaf.

Makes about 11 cups or 8 servings.

PAUL SCHELL
WATERMARK TOWER
1904
1107 FIRST AVENUE
SEATTLE, WASHINGTON 98101

SALMON WITH THREE-MUSTARD SAUCE

1 cup Fish Fumet
  or stock
	1 heaping tablespoon
	  Pommery mustard

1/2 cup dry white wine	1 heaping tablespoon tarragon mustard

4 (6 to 8-ounce) fresh
  salmon fillets
	1 teaspoon chopped
	  fresh tarragon

1-1/2 cups heavy cream	1 tablespoon butter, cold
1 heaping tablespoon Dijon mustard	

1. Preheat the oven to 200 degrees.

2. In a large frying pan, heat the fish fumet and white wine until simmering. Add the salmon fillets, skin side up. Simmer the salmon for 3 to 5 minutes, then turn over.

3. Discard 1/2 cup of the fumet and add the cream. Bring the mixture to a slow boil. Boil gently for 3 to 4 minutes, or until the fish is firm.

4. Remove the salmon and place in a shallow boat dish; place in the preheated oven until ready to serve.

5. Continue reducing the cream sauce until it thickens enough to cling to the salmon when served. Add the mustards and the tarragon. Blend together over low heat until incorporated.

6. Add the cold butter to finish the sauce. Remove the pan from the heat and swirl the sauce until the butter has melted. Pour over the salmon and serve.

Formula

ITEM   HOLIDAY FRUIT STOLLEN

FROM: BILL SCHUMACHER

PAGE

INGREDIENTS	LBS.	OZS.	BLENDING METHOD
BREAD FLOUR	4	14	1. Cream butter, shortening, salt, malt and sugar.
WATER (VARIABLE)	2		2. Add the eggs gradually.
YEAST		6	3. Dissolve the yeast in a portion of the water.
SALT		1	4. Dissolve the milk powder in the remainder of the water and add to the creamed ingredients in No. 1.
MALT		1	
GRANULATED SUGAR		12	
MILK POWDER		4	5. Add the flavorings and the flour. Mix to a smooth firm dough.
BUTTER OR MARGARINE		9	6. Allow dough one full rise, then place dough back on the mixer and add the washed and drained fruit.
SHORTENING		9	
WHOLE EGGS		4	
EGG YOLKS		4	7. Mix only long enough to fully incorporate the fruit. Place dough on floured bench and divide.
RUM FLAVOR		1/2	
MACE		1/4	
FRESH LEMON GRATINGS		1/4	8. Scale or divide into 16 to 18 oz. pieces; round up and form into oval shape and allow 20 to 25 minutes to recover before shaping.
MIXED FRUIT	4	1	
PECAN PIECES		4	

9. Roll out the center of each piece using a small rolling pin. Wash centers with melted butter and fold in the shape of a large Parkerhouse roll.
10. Place straight, or form into crescent shape on pans.
11. Give medium-full proof without steam.
12. Oven temperature, 400° F.; 415°F.; baking time is approximately 30 minutes.
13. YIELD: Approximately 14 @ 1 lb. ea.

SUGGESTED: Wash with melted butter while hot and dust with powdered sugar when cool.

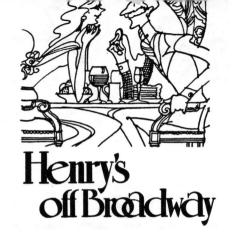

Henry's off Broadway

John Henry Schwartz

Over the years, this recipe for Chicken Sesame Salad has been one of the most popular items on our menus. We have been asked for the recipe again and again by those people visiting our restaurants, and we're pleased to be sharing it with you in order to benefit Children's Orthopedic.

CHICKEN SESAME SALAD

(Serves 2)

2 heads Romaine Lettuce
¼ cup Toasted Slivered Almonds
¼ cup diced Celery
¼ cup Cooking Oil

1½ cups cooked, shredded
  Chicken Breast
2 Tbsp. Toasted Sesame Seeds
2 Wonton Wrappers
1 cup Sweet & Sour Dressing

Romaine lettuce should be washed clean, all dark leaves and core removed. Steam chicken meat 5 minutes or until done. Cool and slice thin, julienne style. In small frying pan on medium heat, fry wonton wrappers in cooking oil one at a time until crisp. Remove from pan and drain off excess oil. Cool.

In large mixing bowl, put lettuce, cooked chicken meat, celery, almonds, 1 Tbsp. toasted sesame seeds. Crumble fried wonton wrappers with hand into salad. Toss well. Add dressing to salad and toss well again.

Divide salad onto 2 chilled plates or bowls. Top salads with remaining 1 Tbsp. sesame seeds. Garnish with tomato or lemon wedges.

SWEET & SOUR DRESSING

2 cups Sugar
1½ cups Rice Wine Vinegar
2 tsp. peeled, grated fresh Ginger
2 Tbsp. Sesame Oil
1 Tbsp. Lemon Juice
1½ tsp. Salt

4 tsp. Colman's Dry Mustard
2 Tbsp. Soy Sauce
1 clove Garlic, minced
4 Tbsp. Vegetable Oil
2 tsp. cracked Black Pepper

Sift together sugar and mustard. Slowly add vinegar until smooth consistency. Place mixture in top of double boiler. Cook and stir until sugar dissolves.

Stir in soy sauce, ginger, garlic. Blend well. Stir in both oils, lemon juice, salt and pepper. Remove from stove, cool and refrigerate 4 hours to allow flavors time to blend. NOTE: Stir well before use.

John Henry Schwartz

Department of Sociology, DK–40
Pepper Schwartz

I pick recipes according to two principles: the likelihood of an ooh and aah--and how quick it is to put together. If there is a competition between the two principles, the second is by far the more powerful.

I love this recipe, given by a friend who was taking Italian cooking lessons, because it can be kept in cans, on a shelf, instantly ready for service if company drops by. I like the ability to be spontaneous about inviting someone over - or gracious if they happen to appear. Hence I have a number of "canned" menus that are dear to me. This one is an appetizer-but beware. It is so addictive and wonderful that sometimes we just kept making it over and over and never got to the main course.

Olive Spread

You need:

Crackers-or preferably, toasted fresh french bread, thinly sliced.
One can pitted black olives.
Half cup very good quality olive oil-the better the oil, the better the spread.
Anchovies--this is personal. Three are OK--but if you love salt, then you can do
*   as I do--put five or six in.*
A teaspoon or so of chopped onion.
A few sprigs of fresh parsley (you can use dried but there is no comparison to
*   the fresh)*
Garlic--like the anchovies, this is best defined by how much you love the stuff.
*   I use two sections--but I have been known to be excessive and use three.*

You take all this stuff, throw it in a blender--whirl it around a few moments-- if you like it very smooth you whirl it around a minute or so. I like it sort of lumpy so I blend it very briefly. That's it. It is enough for four to six people to have several tastes, but I warn you that few people will be able to restrain themselves and have a moderate amount. I would say double the recipe for most groups.

UNIVERSITY OF WASHINGTON
SEATTLE, WASHINGTON 98105

Police Department

I am happy to forward to you a recipe for Poppy Seed French Bread.
It has become a favorite of our large extended family, as well as
visiting law enforcement colleagues from throughout the United States
and of course our friends and neighbors. It could also be known as
"Magical Disappearing Poppy Seed Bread" because great amounts of it
disappear immediately in the buffet serving setting. Our experience
has been that with certain popular items you double what would be a
normal portion. This has proven to be one of those situations.

POPPY SEED FRENCH BREAD

1 large unsliced loaf french bread
1 cup butter
½ tsp. paprika
1 tsp. poppy seeds
¼ tsp. garlic powder

Trim all the crust from the bread except the bottom crust,
slice down the center of the loaf lengthwise, being careful
not to cut through the bottom crust. Then cut across bread
in ½ inch slices - still being careful not to cut through the
bottom crust. Melt butter in saucepan and add paprika, garlic,
and poppy seeds. Using a pastry brush, brush butter mix onto
bread, down the center lengthwise, then across, then over top
and sides of bread. Wrap in foil until ready to bake. At this
point bread may be frozen. When ready to bake, roll foil down
the sides of bread to form a pan and bake in preheated oven
400 degrees for 15 minutes.

This bread is a great companion with barbecued meats; however, it seems to
also go well with a wide variety of menus. A final word of caution. Make
sure teenage males come at the end of the buffet line as they seem to
inhale Poppy Seed Bread. Good luck!

Sincerely,

Michael G. Shanahan
Chief of Police

1117 Northeast Boat Street, HE-10 / Telephone: (206) 543-9331

Gerard M. Shellan

Seattle, Washington
98104

ALMOND CHEESECAKE

1 lb. cream cheese at room temperature
2/3 c. plus 3 Tbsp. sugar
3 eggs
3/4 tsp. almond extract
1 pt. sour cream
1 tsp. vanilla extract

Place cream cheese, 2/3 cup sugar, eggs and
almond extract in electric mixer; beat until
smooth, light and lemon colored. Pour into
buttered 8 inch cake pan. Bake 30 to 35
minutes at 325 degrees. Remove from oven;
let cool for 20 minutes. Mix sour cream,
remaining sugar and vanilla; spread on
cheesecake. Put in oven for 10 to 15 minutes.
Remove; sprinkle with thinly sliced almonds.

9-10 servings

Gerard M. Shellan

Allen C. Shoup
President

Chateau Ste Michelle

One Stimson Lane
Woodinville, Washington 98072
206/488-1133

VEAL STROGANOFF
serves 6

1-1/2 lbs. boneless veal stew meat (cut in 1½" cubes)
3 Italian sausages (cut in 1" slices)
2 T. olive oil
1 medium onion, chopped
2 garlic cloves, minced
1/2 lb. fresh mushrooms, halved
1 c. beef broth
1 red bell pepper, seeded and chopped
1/2 c. dry white wine
1 bay leaf
1 T. parsley, finely chopped
1/2 t. salt
pepper to taste
1 c. sour cream
2 T. flour
hot cooked noodles

Heat oil in dutch oven over medium-high heat; add meats
and brown well on all sides. Stir in onion, garlic and
mushrooms; saute. Add broth, bell pepper, wine, bay
leaf, parsley, salt and pepper; stir well. Bring to
boil, cover, reduce heat and simmer for approximately 1½
hours. Turn heat to high, cook uncovered until liquid is
reduced to about one cup. In small bowl mix sour cream
and flour until thoroughly blended and stir into veal
mixture. Cook stirring continually for 3-4 minutes.
Serve over hot cooked noodles.

Seattle City Council

Norman B. Rice
President of the City Council
625-2436

George E. Benson
Chair
Transportation Committee
625-2441

Virginia Galle
Chair
Environmental Management
Committee
625-2445

Michael Hildt
Chair
Energy Committee
625-2443

Paul Kraabel
Chair
Urban Redevelopment
Committee and Public
Safety Committee
625-2447

Dolores Sibonga
Chair
Finance Committee
625-2451

Sam Smith
Chair
Housing, Recreation &
Human Services Committee
625-2455

Jim Street
Chair
Land Use Committee
625-2438

Jeanette Williams
Chair
City Operations Committee
625-2453

Quick & Easy Teriyaki

3 lbs. cut-up chicken
2 c. Kikkoman marinade
2 T. brown sugar
2 T. salad oil

Mix all ingredients and marinate for at least an hour. Place on cookie sheet and bake 1 to 1½ hours at 300°.

Dolores Sibonga

An equal employment opportunity—affirmative action employer
Eleventh Floor, Municipal Building, Seattle, Washington 98104

133

SEATTLE
SUPERSONICS

P.O. Box 900911
Seattle, WA 98109-9711

JOE'S SPECIAL

1 lb. ground beef
1 chopped onion
1 cup fresh grated parmesan
2 eggs
2 10 oz. pkgs. chopped spinach, cooked and drained.

Brown ground beef and onion, drain off excess fat.

Mix all together saving parmesan for last.

Serve with french bread.

Jack and Shawn Sikma

SEATTLE POLICE DEPARTMENT MEMORANDUM

TO   Children's Orthopedic Hospital & Medical Center   **DATE**

FROM   Assistant Chief Noreen Skagen
Field Support Bureau   **PAGE**   **OF**

SUBJECT   FAVORITE RECIPE

STRAWBERRY CREAM PIE

Vanilla Wafer Crust -

1½ cups fine vanilla crumbs (save 2 tbl. for trim)
1/3 cup melted butter

Press into 9" pie pan. Chill until firm - 45 minutes.

Filling -

1/2 cup butter
1½ cups powdered sugar
2   beaten eggs

Beat until fluffy. Spoon into crust.

Fold -

1½ cups whipping cream (whipped)
1½ cups sliced strawberries

Spread over egg mixture. Chill until firm.

FRIED RICE (Chow Fon)

6 Cups cold cooked rice:
>   2 cups long grain white rice
>   2 cups cold water, 1 cup chicken broth, ½ tsp. salt

Rinse rice in strainer under cold water rubbing gently until clean - let rest in strainer one hour. Use 4-5 quart lidded pot; add above ingredients and bring to rolling boil. Cover and reduce to simmer for 15 minutes. Set aside 20 minutes without removing cover; then lift lid and fluff with fork; let stand till cool, then seal and refrigerate overnight.

1 Cup chicken breast cut into ¼" cubes and marinated overnight with 2 egg whites blended with ½ tsp. salt, 1 tbs. cornstarch and 1 tbs. rice wine.

1 Cup loin pork diced in ¼" cubes and marinated overnight with 3 tbs. soy sauce, 1 tbs. rice wine, 1 tbs. honey and 1 tbs. lemon juice.

2 Eggs beaten with ½ tsp. salt and 1 tbs. water; cooked as thin omelet in flat skillet with 1 tsp. butter - set aside.

2 Cups fresh (or frozen) peas - put in strainer and dip for 45 seconds in large pot of boiling water with ½ tsp. salt and 1 tbs. corn oil, immediately immerse in ice water - set aside.

Place chicken in strainer and squeeze out marinade. Shake to loosen. Immerse in boiling water with 1 tbs. corn oil and ½ tsp. salt for 40 seconds, then immediately immerse in ice water - set aside. Place Pork in strainer and squeeze out marinade. Immerse in boiling water with 1 tbs. corn oil and ½ tsp. salt for 60 seconds then immediately immerse in ice water - set aside.

Chop or dice the following in ¼" cubes:

1/2 cup cooked lean ham	1/3 cup celery	1/2 cup cashews
2/3 cup red bell pepper	1/2 cup green onions	1/4 cup raisins
2/3 cup green bell pepper	1 cup bean sprouts	1/2 cup almonds

In a large skillet or wok, place 2 tbs. corn oil, 1 garlic clove (mashed), 1 tsp. grated fresh ginger, 1 tsp. finely chopped green onion and 1/8 tsp. dried red chile flakes. Stir and when garlic begins to brown, add chicken and stir for 60 seconds. Remove with slotted spoon and drain in strainer over pan - set aside. Add almonds and cashews. Stir until golden. Remove with slotted spoon and set aside on paper toweling.

Add pork to skillet and stir for 2 minutes. Remove with slotted spoon, drain and set aside. Return drained oil from chicken and pork to skillet. Add red & green pepper to skillet and stir for 10 seconds. Add green onions and celery and stir for 10 seconds. Add almonds, raisins, bean sprouts, ham and stir for 30 seconds. Remove with slotted spoon and drain in strainer over pan - set aside. (If in doubt cook less, not more). Stirfry rice in large skillet with 2 tbs. oil hot enough to sizzle grain of rice. Toss and separate as much as possible for 2-3 minutes. If sticking add 1-1½ tsp oil. Add 2 tsp. coarse (Kosher) salt when hot - toss. Add cooked vegetables, nuts and meat - toss. Add peas - toss. Add 1 tbs. oyster sauce -toss. Cut egg omelet into strips ¼" wide x 1" long - add, and also add ¼ cup hot chicken broth - toss thoroughly.

Serve or can be held, covered, in 200º oven for a while. Also great warmed over, the next day. Serves 8-10.

John B. Skilling
John B. Skilling
Chairman & C.E.O.

JOHN B. SKILLING	WILLIAM D. WARD	KENT R. ROGERS	ARTHUR J. BARKSHIRE	JON D. MAGNUSSON
FRANK W. HOELTERHOFF	MICHAEL B. RIGO	ROBERT P. ST. GERMAIN	JACK L. GUISE	RAMON D. UPSAHL	J. WESTON HALL
JOSE P. ALMA JOSE	SERGE RUDCHENKO	RICHARD E. TAYLOR	AD A. GOUWEROK	ICHIRO IKEDA	MARY ANN MILLER
JOSTEIN NES	FIRMAN W. GUENTHER	DONALD K. BARG	E. ANN FERRESE	STEPHEN D. HANSEN
JOHN T. LEVESQUE	JANET F. VAN ZANT	STANLEY W. RAWSON	TONY TSCHANZ	JOHN V. CHRISTIANSEN-CONSULTANT

SEATTLE   ANCHORAGE   SAN FRANCISCO

A. V. Smith
President

Pacific Northwest Bell

1600 Bell Plaza, Room 3101
Seattle, Washington 98191
Phone (206) 345-3223

WALNUT SOLE

Serves 2

1/4 cup fine cracker crumbs
3/4 cup white flour
2 filets of sole (or more depending on size)
2 egg whites, beaten stiff
1 cup sliced walnuts (not chopped)
4 tablespoons butter

Mix cracker crumbs and flour together in plastic
sack. Shake fish in bag to coat, shake off excess.
Dip filets in egg whites, then in bowl of walnut
meats. Be sure to cover fish well with nuts.
Heat heavy pan and melt butter over low heat.
Fry filets slowly over low heat 5 - 10 minutes,
depending on size of filets.

CANDIED YAMS

4 medium yams
¼ lb. butter (one stick)
1/3 cup brown sugar
3/4 cup crushed pineapple

Peel and cut length-wise the yams. Boil until tender but still firm.

Place in a med-high frying pan and add all ingredients.

Cook until all liquid is absorbed by potatoes and then fry until close to "burning." (Will be a brown/black)

You can bake the potatoes at 300 for 45 minutes but it is not the traditional way and the "burning" gives the yams the crispy,sweet flavor.

Ricky and Dianne Sobers

THE WORLD'S GREATEST MACARONI AND CHEESE

1½ cups macaroni
½ lb. butter
1 lb. sharp cheddar cheese
2 cans evaporated milk
salt to taste (about 2 t)

Preheat oven to 350º.
Boil macaroni in lots of water until it is al dente,
about 6 minutes, and place in a casserole dish. (To
measure the casserole dish, place dry macaroni inside
it. It should be 1/3 full.)

Dice the butter and cheese. Mix butter, cheese, milk,
and salt with cooked macaroni. Cook in the oven until
the cheese and butter are melted. Mix thoroughly until
the cheese, butter and milk are totally amalgamated.
The milk should just cover the macaroni mixture.

Allow it to cook without further stirring until the
top has formed a golden brown crust, about 45 minutes.

Bill Speidel

E.M.M. Northwest Harvest
711 Cherry Street • P.O. Box 12272
Seattle, WA 98102
(206) 625-0755

This is from a collection of recipes which Northwest Harvest makes
available to food bank users. The recipes emphasize low-cost ingredients while
resulting in tasty and nutritious dishes.

BEANS AND RICE MEDLEY

½ lb. dried beans, your choice
¼ lb. rice
1 large onion, finely chopped
3 stalks celery, finely chopped
4 tbsp. olive oil (or any vegetable oil)

2 fresh tomatoes, peeled and chopped
1 hot chili pepper, finely chopped
Salt
3 English muffins, halved

<u>WASH</u> beans. Soak beans in water overnight. Or, for quick-soak method, bring
beans and hot water to boil; boil 2 minutes, remove from heat, cover and let
stand 1 hour. Cook beans in plenty of water -- about 1½ to 2 hours -- seasoned
with salt only. When tender, place aside in their own liquid.
<u>SAUTE</u> onion and celery in oil until golden brown, then add the tomatoes and
pepper. Cook together, stirring often, for 10 minutes and add to the beans.
Heat the beans until the boiling point is reached, add the rice and cook until
rice is tender. Keep the liquid to the desired consistency of thick soup.
Serve over English muffins. Serves 6.

Ruth M. Sterling

Fresh Bean Sprout Salad

3 cups fresh bean sprouts, rinsed and drained
1 cup julienne-cut cucumber
1 cup julienne-cut celery
2 cups julienne-cut cooked chicken
½ cup chopped green onion
Bibb Lettuce

Sesame Dressing

1 teaspoon sugar
½ teaspoon salt
½ teaspoon paprika
¼ teaspoon dry mustard
Freshly ground pepper to taste
1 clove garlic, crushed
½ cup salad oil
1 tablespoon white wine vinegar
3 tablespoons toasted sesame seeds
1 tablespoon sesame seed oil

In glass bowl combine bean sprouts, cucumber, celery, chicken and green onion.

For dressing, blend dry ingredients; add garlic and oils, mixing well. Add vinegar and sesame seeds; beat or shake well.

Pour over sprout mixture, stirring to coat thoroughly with dressing.

Cover and refrigerate several hours.

Pile on top of bibb lettuce leaves to serve.

Bobbie Stern

Bobbie Stern has served on the Board of Directors of the Puget Sound Chapter of the March of Dimes and on the Board of the Junior League of Seattle. She is on the Board of Trustees of Cornish Institute and is serving as Development Co-Chairman of Seattle Central Community College's Foundation. Bobbie is a founding director of the Mercer Island Community Fund and is on the National Board of Directors of City of Hope Medical and Research Center.

In addition, Bobbie has the distinction of being the only member of the Mercer Island Cooking Contest Hall of Fame for her culinary skill!

Tom Stockley's
WINE NOTES

Tom Stockley, The Seattle Times wine columnist and food writer, lives on a Lake Union houseboat with his wife, Peggy. He developed this recipe originally for Lake Union crayfish but, as they are not available year-round, he adapted it to prawns usually found in the Pike Place Market or other local seafood outlets.

PRONTO PRAWNS IN PERNOD
(Four servings)

24 large raw shrimp or prawns, shelled and deveined
4 tablespoons unsalted butter
1 clove garlic, chopped into about four pieces
1/4 cup Pernod
2/3 cup heavy or raw cream
Salt and pepper to taste
Parsley for garnish

   1. Advance preparation: Shell and devein the seafood early in day for easy cooking at serving time.

   2. Over medium heat, melt the butter in a large skillet and quickly saute the seafood with the garlic until they turn pink (about four minutes).

   3. Pour the Pernod into the pan and ignite with long fireplace match or kitchen match; stand back from pan to avoid injury. As soon as flames die down, remove the seafood from the pan and keep warm on a serving platter. Discard garlic.

   4. Turn up heat to high and pour cream into the pan. Cook for about four minutes until reduced and well mixed with Pernod and butter. Taste for seasonings. Pour sauce over seafood and serve; garnish with parsley.

BEER WAFFLES

My love for waffles began years ago when my mother and grandmother prepared them from scratch on Sunday mornings. Years later, when I started making them myself, I discovered this simple recipe for beer waffles, which are much lighter and crisper than conventional waffles.

1 12-ounce can of Rainier Beer (or any similar brew)
1 1/2 cups all-purpose flour
4 fresh eggs
2 tablespoons corn oil
2 tablespoons melted butter
1 tablespoon sugar
1/4 teaspoon fresh-ground cinnamon

Set waffle iron on medium and allow to preheat.

Combine flour, sugar and cinnamon in small mixing bowl. Break eggs into another mixing bowl and add oil, melted butter and beer (light American beers are fine, but try experimenting with more exotic brews).

Beat mixture with a wire whisk for about two minutes, then add flour, sugar and cinnamon (a sifter helps). Thoroughly stir all ingredients before transferring to a large pitcher. Batter will be pretty thin.

If waffle iron doesn't have non-stick surfaces, brush top and bottom with non-burning vegetable oil. Pour enough batter into waffle iron to completely cover bottom. Cook until steaming stops, about three to five minutes.

Serve piping hot with heated maple syrup and butter, or fresh, sliced strawberries and dollops of whipped cream. Isernio's hot Italian-style sausage and fresh Starbuck's coffee make excellent accompaniments.

Gene Stout

Gene Stout

Althea Stroum

GLAZED CHICKEN

```
4 whole broiler-fryer breasts, boned
1 cup flour              1 tsp curry powder
1 tsp ground nutmeg      ½ tsp salt
¼ tsp pepper             3 Tbs parve margarine
3 Tbs sherry type wine   1 can (8¼ oz.) seedless
4 Tbs orange marmalade     grapes
```

Mix flour with curry powder, nutmeg, salt and

pepper. Dip chicken breasts in seasoned flour,

coat evenly. Heat margarine in heavy skillet

over medium heat; add chicken; brown, turning as

needed. Reduce heat and continue cooking about

twenty minutes or until tender. Just before

serving, pour in wine and simmer few minutes.

Push chicken to one side of skillet and warm

grapes. Add marmalade and toss gently.

Sincerely,
Althea Stroum

KAY'S APPLE KUCHEN

Preheat Oven to 350 degrees

Ingredients For Crust

1 Stick Butter (Softened)
1 Yellow Cake Mix
1/2 Cup Coconut (Flaked)

Cut butter into cake mix. Stir in coconut. Pat into a 9 x 13
metal pan and bake 10 minutes at 350 degrees. (Note:
You must use a metal pan or the crust will not set as well.)

Ingredients For Filling

2 1/2 Cups Apples (Two apples, peeled and sliced)
1/4 Cup Sugar
1 Teaspoon Cinnamon
1 Cup Sour Cream
1 Egg

Arrange sliced apples on warm crust (no need to cool). Sprinkle
cinnamon/sugar mixture over apples. Blend sour cream and egg
together and drizzle the mixture on top of the apples.

Bake at 350 degrees for 25 minutes. Cool overnight before
serving. Cut into 12 dessert servings or 2 inch squares for
cookie servings, whichever you prefer and ENJOY, ENJOY, ENJOY!!!

This recipe was selected from among the very best specialties
that are prepared by and for our employees for our annual Holiday
party. Guaranteed to peel off several pounds for the diet con-
scious! With best wishes from all of us at Jay Jacobs, ENJOY!

Douglas A. Swerland
President

145

LOU TICE - THE PACIFIC INSTITUTE

<u>Baked</u> <u>Salmon</u> <u>Elegante'</u>

1 10-pound white King Salmon, filleted and boned (2 pieces)
3 Cups Best Foods Mayonnaise

Preheat oven to 425 F.

Spread mayonnaise heavily on each fillet. Place on pan (deep cookie sheet) in opposite directions.

Bake at 425 F. for 15 minutes. Very moist.

Serves 15.

Cook's note: In our business, we often have 15 people at a moment's notice. This is a favorite recipe of Diane's for a quick, elegant dinner. Usually we serve it with new potatoes browned in butter and sprinkled with parsely, and two kinds of colorful vegetables, quickly steamed.

Rainier National Bank
Box 3966, Seattle, Washington 98124, (206) 621-4244

G. Robert Truex, Jr.
Chairman

Roast Rack of Lamb Dijon

Pre-heat oven to 350°

1 rack of lamb - 6-8 ribs

olive oil

1 clove garlic - crushed

1 cup good beef stock (preferably homemade)

3/4 cup dry white wine

dash thyme

6 T's butter

1 cup bread crumbs

3 shallots, chopped

1/4 cup chopped parsley

1/4 cup Dijon mustard

salt and pepper to taste

Make small cut between ribs on back to ease carving later, and tie ribs securely with string. In an oven-proof pan, sear rack on all sides in olive oil. Remove lamb. In same pan, gently fry garlic. Add stock, wine and thyme, scraping crusty bits from bottom. Return rack to pan and bake at 350° for 40 minutes or until pink, basting occasionally. Remove lamb and keep warm. Quickly reduce sauce to approximately 3/4 cup. While lamb is cooking, saute bread crumbs and shallots in butter until lightly browned, about 3-5 minutes. Stir in parsley. Spread mustard on top of lamb, pat breadcrumbs over top and put under broiler for 1 to 2 minutes. Remove string from lamb and carve into 1 or 2 bone ribs. Spoon sauce on each serving plate, place lamb on top and serve hot.

Serves 4

RAINIERBANK

147

John and I have odd working hours, and a three
year old, (another child is on the way). I'd rather
be reading to my little girl than slicing and dicing
in the kitchen. It always makes me sigh to see how
much time some so-called quick-and-easy recipes expect
me to spend cooking. These recipes are <u>really</u> fast.

<u>QUICK SCALLOPS</u>: Saute fresh, minced garlic in butter.
Add the scallops and just a little white wine, and
saute for 10 minutes or so. Serve with rice and a
salad.

<u>BROILED CHICKEN</u>: Remove the skin from chicken pieces,
place them on a broiling pan, and baste with low-
calorie Italian dressing. Broil until lightly browned;
turn, and baste and broil again. Then let bake for
20 minutes, or until you're ready to eat.

<u>SHRIMP AND PEAS</u>: Stir fry without the slicing!
Stir fry 3/4ths of a pound of shrimp in hot oil in
a wok. Remove shrimp, add a little more oil to the
wok. When that's hot, throw in a slice of ginger
root and two cloves of minced garlic. Then add 10
ounces of tiny peas (frozen ones are fine; they'll
cook more quickly if they're thawed, but it isn't
crucial). When the peas are tender, put the shrimp
back in, add a glop of rice wine, and stir fry a
minute until it's all hot. Serves two very generously,
with rice.

<u>CHAMPAGNE AND ORANGE JUICE</u>: We have a lot of weekend
company, and champagne and orange juice served together in pretty stemmed glasses make even scrambled
eggs festive. (And NOTHING is faster than scrambled
eggs).

<u>MELON AND SHERBET</u>: An easy dessert. My favorite combin-
ation is wedges of honeydew filled with raspberry
sherbet. Serve with store-bought butter cookies.

Gina Tuttle
KOMO Radio News Anchor

ZOLLIE M. VOLCHOK
2920 - 76TH AVENUE S. E. ● MERCER ISLAND, WASHINGTON 98040

KAN'S LAMB CHINESE

2 pounds lean lamb cut in 1½ inch cubes

Marinade

     ¼ cup Hoisin sauce
     2 Tablespoons Soy
     2 Tablespoons Sugar
     2 Tablespoons Cornstarch
     2 Tablespoons Oil
     2 Small Cloves of Garlic, Minced
     2 Tablespoons Sesame Oil
     2 Tablespoons of Sherry
     1/8 th Tablespoon White Pepper

Combine all ingredients and marinate lamb mixing well. Cover with plastic and refrigerate over night.

Heat oil and stir fry until brown. Add 2 tablespoons of dark soy sauce and 2 tablespoons of sugar and stir fry 30 seconds more.

Serve over rice sticks or rice.

Will serve from 4 to 6.

RUTH'S CHICKEN

(This family recipe, as in most Southern families, has been passed down from generation to generation. I don't know how old the recipe is, but I've been eating it all my life!)

4 boned chicken breasts	dash of paprika
1 to 1-1/4 lb. asparagus, trimmed*	1 tsp. curry (to taste)
1 can cream of chicken soup	1/2 C mayonnaise
1 cup sharp cheddar cheese	1 Tbsp. butter
white pepper to taste	juice of 1/2 lemon

*if you prefer, use broccoli or brussels sprouts.

Saute boned chicken in butter (undercook it to brown). Take breast out, drain and let stand.

Blanch or microwave asparagus (keep crisp). 4-min. high

Warm baking dish in oven. Put asparagus all around the dish, heads up, in a decorative fashion.

Place chicken breasts in center of asparagus. Mix together soup, mayonnaise, white pepper, curry and lemon juice. Pour mixture over chicken breasts and asparagus.

Sprinkle cheese over top. Bake at 350 for 25-minutes.

Sprinkle paprika and serve.

Serves 4.

RUTH WALSH

1620 S. Lk. Stickney Dr., Lynnwood, WA 98037
A division of Pacific Video Communications, Inc.

© All Rights R

MARILYN B. WARD

DINNER ISLAND STIR FRY

Vegetable oil - 3 to 4 Tbls.
Shrimp - 1 pound, shelled
Broccoli - 1 medium head, flowers and stems cut into small pieces
    and blanched
Onion - 1 medium, sliced thin
Green and Red Peppers - 1/4 each, finely sliced
Celery - 2 medium stalks sliced thinly on the diagonal
Tomato - 1 large or 2 medium, peeled and chopped roughly
Parsley - 1 Tbls. coarsely chopped
Salt, pepper to taste
Lemon juice - 1 to 2 Tbls.
Fettuccine or thin Spaghetti - 4 ounces

Put oil in wok or saute pan or frying pan and when heated, saute onion
until transparent.
Add shrimp and stir fry until pink.
Add celery, blanched broccoli, green and red peppers and stir fry
1 to 2 minutes.
Add tomatoes, parsley, lemon juice, salt and pepper and cook until
tomatoes are heated through.
Toss with cooked fettuccine.
Serves four.

Crusty french bread, a tossed green salad with vinaigrette dressing
and a good cold dry white wine goes well with this.

Marilyn Ward is a founding director of Sound Savings and Loan and
founding governor and first president of Cityclub. She has also
served as vice-president of the Metropolitan Board of the Seattle
YMCA and is a past president of the Visiting Committee of the School
of Social Work at the University of Washington.

Officers

President
Mr. James F. Brinkley, Jr.

Vice Presidents
Mrs. Robert Denny Watt
Mr. Robert C. Wing
Mrs. John Mangels

Treasurer
Mr. John H. Davis

Assistant Treasurer
Mr. Keith James

Secretary
Mr. David L. Williams

Trustees
Mrs. Durwood Alkire
Mr. William Borah
Mrs. Robert F. Buck
Mr. Luther J. Carr
Mr. A. H. Clise
Mrs. George W. Corley
Mr. Michael Dederer
Mr. Robert Dickey
Mrs. Doyle E. Fowler
Mr. Andrew J. Harris
Mr. Philip G. Johnson
Mr. Roy W. Morse
Mr. H. W. McCurdy
Mr. Robert B. McEachern
Mr. Bernard B. Pelly
Mr. William M. Polk
Mr. Robert Roblee
Mr. John N. Rupp
Mr. Hoge Sullivan
Mr. D. P. Van Blaricom
Mr. D. K. Weaver, Sr.
Mr. S. M. Wetherald

Museum Director
Dr. James R Warren

CORN CHOWDER

8 ozs. bacon, rendered
2 onions, chopped
½ cup chopped celery tops
½ bay leaf, crumbled
2 tablespoons flour
Salt & pepper
Chopped parsley
Paprika

3 cups diced potato
2 cans cream style corn
2 cups evaporated milk (or
    half & half/or milk to equal)
4 cups water (if milk is used
    above, reduce amount of wate

Render bacon and remove from pan and pour off all but
3 tablespoons fat. Add onions and celery tops and cook
5 minutes. Blend in flour. Add water and potato;
bring to boil and simmer, covered, 15 minutes. Add corn
and milk; heat well. Season. Add paprika and serve with
parsley and paprika.

Sincerely

James R Warren
Director, MOHAI

HISTORICAL SOCIETY OF SEATTLE AND KING COUNTY
2700 - 24th AVENUE EAST, McCURDY PARK, SEATTLE, WASHINGTON 98112, (206) 324-1125

KATE B. WEBSTER
15369 BROOM ST. N.E.
BAINBRIDGE ISLAND, WA. 98110

RE: RECIPE FROM KATE WEBSTER

CREAMY RUM PIE

1 - 10" Cookie Crumb crust (vanilla cookies)

6 - large egg yolks
1/2 - cup water (cold)
1 - tablespoon gelatin (plain)
7/8 - cup sugar (almost a cup)
1/3 - cup dark rum
1 - pint whipping cream

2 - squares bittersweet chocolate - grated

Beat yolks and sugar until thick and lemon colored
Place water and gelatin in a small pan -- heat
   slowly until it starts to simmer
Pour into yolk mixture beating constantly -- add rum
Whip cream into creamy peaks, fold into the mixture
Pour into cooked crust
Sprinkle grated chocolate on top -- cool in refrigerator
   for at least four (4) hours (or overnight)
This pie freezes well

We served Creamy Rum Pie to Julia Child in 1974. She
asked for a second helping!

Kate B. Webster

Because It's There

SALMON BAR-B-QUE   NORTHWEST NATIVE AMERICAN STYLE

Build an Alderwood fire and let burn at least one hour allowing good coals to develop. Dig a hole in the ground to accomodate the stick you will be using to support the salmon over your fire.

Take fresh salmon and clean, removing head and slicing open front of fish all the way to tail. Remove backbone leaving back of fish (skin) intact so the two filets will hold together.

Whittle or split approximately 12 (depending on size of fish) sticks of cedar, ¼" by 12". Make one large stick 2" by 6' and split in half for two feet of its length.

Insert the fish into the split so that the stick is on each side of the back skin and lay on flat surface so one filet extends on either side of the stick. Secure split to prevent further widening with honeysuckle vine (you might cheat here and use coat hanger wire, etc.). Weave in small sticks to support the filets, and secure top of big stick with more vine.

Paint a mixture of lemon, olive oil, butter, garlic, salt and pepper onto fish.

Insert stick into ground angling salmon well above coals with skin side on top. Cook slowly for 30 minutes and rotate. Test fish with splinter until done. It will be soft, moist and delicious.

I have cooked six salmon on one fire using this method, and I dream about eating it on my mountain climbing expeditions.

Jim Whittaker

Whittaker/O'Malley, Inc.
Expedition quality clothing
and equipment

1000 First Avenue South
Seattle, Washington 98134
(206) 382-0455

P.O. Box 4266
Pioneer Square Station
Seattle, Washington 98104

SEATTLE SUPERSONICS

P.O. Box 900911
Seattle, WA 98109-9711

ARTICHOKE CRAB DIP

1 cup mayo
1 cup freshly grated parmesan
1 can water-packed artichoke hearts, chopped and drained.
1 cup green onions, chopped
½ lb. or more of fresh crab

Mix all together and season with seasoning salt and garlic powder.

Pour into shallow baking dish, sprinkle with cheddar (optional) and bake at 350 for 20 minutes.

Serve with party rye or crackers hot from the oven.

Great hot or cold! May be prepared ahead of time.

Lenny and Marilyn

FAMILY CASSEROLE

1	8-ounce package wide noodles	2	cups small curd cottage cheese
1	tablespoon butter or margarine	1	cup dairy sour cream
11	ounces beef summer sausage, peeled and sliced	1	teaspoon salt
1	teaspoon salt	1/2	cup chopped onions
2	cups (2-8 ounce cans) tomato sauce	2	tablespoons chopped green pepper
2	tablespoons flour	1/4	cup sliced green stuffed olives

Cook noodles according to package directions. Drain. In a skillet, melt
butter or margarine and then brown meat. Drain excess drippings; stir in
tomato sauce, flour and salt; simmer 10 minutes. Mix together cottage cheese,
sour cream, salt, onion, green pepper, and olives. Place half of noodles
in buttered 3-quart baking dish; spread on all the cottage cheese mixture.
_____ half of noodles and cover with beef mixture. Bake in
_____. Let stand for about 10 minutes before serving.

_____ frozen. Makes 6 to 8 servings.

Katherine Wise
_____
Katherine Wise
Home Economist

Wilkens

156

100

Telex: 32-1078

90 Queen Anne Avenue North —

THE CHOCOLATE BAG LADY

PEANUT BUTTER PUBLISHING

CHOCOLATE BAGS:

10 ounces semisweet chocolate, coarsely chopped

4 small paper bags, 3"x 4"x 2", that are lined with a coated surface (bags used for freshly ground coffee work well trimmed to 3" height)

RASPBERRY SAUCE:

1 pint fresh raspberries or two 10-ounce packages frozen raspberries, thawed and drained

2 tablespoons sugar, or 1 tablespoon sugar if using frozen fruit

MOUSSE:

10 ounces white chocolate, coarsely chopped

2 cups heavy cream

1 vanilla bean, split in half lengthwise

2 tablespoons unsalted butter

2 egg yolks

1 tablespoon Kirsch

1 tablespoon orange liqueur

1. **To Make the Mousse:** In a double boiler over hot water melt the white chocolate, stirring frequently.

2. In a saucepan, combine ½ cup cream, the halved vanilla bean, and butter. Bring to a boil over medium heat. Remove from heat. In a bowl, beat egg yolks for about 1 minute.

3. Remove vanilla bean from cream mixture. Pour half of the hot cream over egg yolks and stir well. Return the yolk/cream mixture to the saucepan and cook over medium heat about 30 seconds, stirring constantly until slightly thickened.

4. Using a wire whisk, stir the melted white chocolate into hot cream. Stir in Kirsch and liqueur. Freeze in bowl for 15 minutes. Stir after 8 minutes and return to freezer.

5. Whip remaining 1½ cup cream until thickened. Stir a third of the whipping cream into chocolate mixture, then fold the chocolate mixture into the remaining whipped cream.

6. Cover mousse with plastic wrap and refrigerate 8 hours or overnight.

7. **To Make the Chocolate Bags:** In a double boiler over hot water melt the semisweet chocolate.

8. Open the bags so that the tops form a rectangle and stand them upright on a flat surface. With a small pastry brush, brush chocolate up from the bottom of each bag until the inside of each bag is evenly coated, with a little extra chocolate in each corner.

9. Freeze the bags for 15 minutes, until set.

10. **To Assemble the Bags:** Fill bags with the chocolate mousse to ¼" from top. Cover and freeze 3½ hours until solid.

11. **To Make the Raspberry Sauce:** In a 1-quart saucepan, combine raspberries and sugar. Bring to a gentle boil. Purée in a food processor, strain, and refrigerate.

12. **To Peel the Bags:** Remove the bags from the freezer, peel away the paper, and refrigerate.

13. **To Serve the Mousse:** Spoon an equal amount of raspberry sauce on each dessert plate. Place an upright bag in the middle of each plate.

14. Fill each bag with a few fresh raspberries or strawberries.

   Publisher's Warning: Watch out! People have been known to fall to their knees after trying this.

Elliot & Karen Wolf

9 WESTERN AVENUE • SUITE 401, MARITIME BUILDING • SEATTLE, WA 98104 • (206) 628-6200

SEATTLE
SUPERSONICS

C Box 14102 — Seattle, WA 98114

PIKE PLACE MARKET HOME-STYLE COLLARD GREENS

4 bunches collard greens
2 pieces salt pork

1 tsp. tenderizer
¼ tsp. regular salt
1 tsp. sugar

Wash greens to clean in cold water. Cut stems off of each leaf. Cut up greens into strips. Start approximately ½ pot of water to boil. Add to the boiling water 2 pieces of salt pork. Cook 45 minutes. In a separate pot of water, add cut up greens and bring to a boil. As soon as greens reach boiling point, remove them from stove and pour them into a colander, letting water drain off. Add greens to first pot of water and cooked salt pork. Now add tenderizer, salt, and sugar and cook greens on medium heat until tender (about 2-2½ hours). Serve hot.

Al Wood

Business Office: 206/628-8400   **Ticket Information:** 628-8448   **Season & Group Sales:** 628-8444

419 Occidental Avenue South — Second Floor   Telex 32-1078

HOT SPICY CHICKEN

1½ to 1 3/4 lb boneless chicken thighs
1 bell pepper diced
1-4 hot green pepper (Jalapeno) diced
4 cloves garlic diced
1 medium red onion diced
1 large yellow onion diced
1 bunch green onions diced
¼ cup olive oil
1 pt jar Ragu tomato sauce with onion and garlic
lemon pepper
salt
black pepper
1 cup water

Wash, pat dry and season chicken with spices to taste
Add ½ cup of olive oil to large skillet and heat till hot.
Add chicken, brown quick on all sides and remove from oil.
Add   remaining olive oil and bring to hot. Add bell pepper and

WOODY WOODHOUSE

Mr. Versatility·Vocalist Extraordinaire

garlic and saute till limp. Add yellow and red onion and saute till limp.
Add green onion, tomato sauce and ¼ cup water to deglaze pan. Reduce heat
add chicken and ¼ cup water and simmer till chicken is opaque through out.
Serve with rice.

This is my mom's own recipe.

Chile Rellenos Casserole

1 can whole green chiles (7oz.)
8 oz. of jack cheese, grated
4 eggs
dash of salt
1 pint of sour cream

Wash the chiles and strip the seams if you desire a mild flavor (a la gringo.)
For a zestier flavor, leave the seams in. Line a 9 x 12 inch pan with the
chiles. Spread grated cheese right on chiles. Separate egg whites. Beat
until stiff. Beat yolks, then add to whites. Mix sour cream with the eggs.
Pour the eggs and sour cream right on top of the chiles and cheese.

Heat oven to 325 degrees. Bake until fluffy and light brown (about 20 minutes.)

Tastes great with salsa on top!

Matt Young

SEATTLE'S CELEBRITY CHEFS

If you would like to support Children's Orthopedic Hospital and Medical Center by ordering additional copies, send:

$9.95 per copy plus $1.50 for postage and handling fee (2 or more books, $2.50 postage and handling). Washington State residents must add 7.9% sales tax.

Please send me ____ copies

BILL TO:

Name _____

Address _____

City _____ State ____ Zip _____

SHIP TO:

Name _____

Address _____

City _____ State ____ Zip _____

☐ Payment enclosed   ☐ Charge

Visa # _____ Exp. Date _____

MasterCard # _____ Exp. Date _____

Signature _____

PEANUT BUTTER PUBLISHING

911 Western Avenue, Suite 401, Maritime Building ▪ Seattle, WA 98104 ▪ (206) 628-6200